MW01490728

Directed Reading-Thinking Activities

by
Jane L. Davidson, Ph.D.
Bonnie C. Wilkerson, Ed.D.

Trillium Press
Monroe, New York

DEDICATION

We dedicate this monograph to Russell G. Stauffer, the creator of the DR-TA. May his vision of teaching/learning awaken teachers and students to active inquiry in an environment of respect for the dignity of all individuals.

ACKNOWLEDGEMENTS

The authors wish to extend appreciation to Nancy Padak and Cheryl Troyer for their suggestions and helpful comments regarding the manuscript.

Trillium Press, Inc.
PO Box 209
Monroe NY 10950
(914) 783-2999

Trillium Press
203 College St, Suite 200
Toronto Ontario
M5T 1P9

ISBN: 0-89824-099-9
Printed in the United States of America

TABLE OF CONTENTS

This monograph is about DR-TAs—what they are, how they work, their value in reading instruction, and research that justifies their use. Although DR-TAs have been in use by a limited number of professionals for over two decades, most professionals have just begun to use them. We have devoted large portions of our professional time to helping in the implementation of DR-TAs through staff development activities in schools, demonstrations in classrooms, and presentations at professional reading conferences. We believe that DR-TAs are highly effective in facilitating students' processes of comprehension attainment. We have observed teachers using DR-TAs through the research investigations we've conducted with the collaboration of Nancy Padak from Kent State University. We have also observed numerous classroom teachers trying to implement DR-TAs. We're impressed with the difficulty many teachers have in assuming the DR-TA teacher's role. Sometimes this difficulty stems from an inability to step completely out of the role associated with more traditional Directed Reading Activities. Sometimes DR-TAs are simply not understood by the teacher. DR-TAs provide an alternative to more traditional teacher-directed reading activities—an alternative that focuses on students' problem-solving. We hope that this monograph aids in helping teachers and other professionals develop greater clarity of understanding about DR-TAs and how to implement them. We urge them to continue to grow and develop in professional expertise with DR-TAs with a phrase coined from Russell Stauffer: "Onward, ardently!"

JLD and BCW

CHAPTER I

THE DIRECTED READING-THINKING ACTIVITY

A teacher sits down at one side of a large table. Eight students are already seated at the table. The teacher has passed out copies of a story that they are going to read. The students have been instructed to cover up the bottom half of the page with a blank sheet of paper that the teacher has given to each of them.

"Read down to the end of the first paragraph of this story in order to get your first clues." (Students read.) "What do you think will happen in this story and why do you think so?"

With these sentences, a Directed Reading-Thinking Activity is in process. The teacher knows that the students will be actively involved in the reading-thinking process and that their responses, reflective of the level of their thinking, will be of high quality. This chapter addresses the Directed Reading-Thinking Activity: what it is, how it compares with the traditional Directed Reading Activity, and some critical aspects inherent in its use.

The DR-TA

The Directed Reading-Thinking Activity (Stauffer, 1980) is a global, problem-solving procedure used to facilitate the improvement of students' critical reading-thinking skills. There are five basic steps in the procedure.

I. **Identifying Purposes for Reading:**
Students set individual or group purposes based on clues in the material and their own background of experience.

II. **Adjustment of Rate to Purposes and Material:**
Rate adjustment depends upon the purposes for reading and the complexity and difficulty of the reading material; surveying, skimming, and studying may be involved.

III. **Observing the Reading:**
Teacher assists students who request help and notes their abilities

to adjust rate to purpose and material, to use word identification strategies and to comprehend material.

IV.   **Developing Comprehension:**
Students check their purposes by accepting, rejecting, and/or redefining purposes. This step is cyclical in nature; students repeat this step until the material has been completely read.

V.   **Fundamental Skill-Training Activities:**
Discussion, further reading, additional study, writing—students and teacher share the responsibility for identifying these needs throughout the strategy. The students have input in the decision regarding follow-up activities.

We will examine each of the DR-TA steps in depth. A description of the actions in each step may provide a clearer understanding of the process of comprehension at work in the procedure.

The first step:
The student examines available clues and declares purposes by making predictions about the content of the material. These predictions are based on the student's background experience, the experiences of others in the group, and the content of the material to be read. As students become involved in making predictions (purpose-setting) in a group setting, they become self-committed to the task on both an intellectual and an emotional level (Stauffer, 1969). Self-commitment is a strong motivating force; the student thus has a need to continue reading to determine accuracy of predictions.

The second step:
The student reads the material, sometimes skimming, sometimes studying in order to satisfy his/her purpose that has been established through the process of predicting. "Purposes for reading represent the key element in versatility. The versatile reader adjusts rate of reading according to purposes for reading and to the nature and difficulty of the material being read" (Stauffer, 1969, p 24). As the student adjusts rate according to purpose and the complexity of material, versatility in reading is facilitated naturally.

The third step:
The teacher observes students while they are reading and discussing, noting students' abilities to attain comprehension, make predictions and support them with information from the text as well as their own background experi-

ence, adjust rate, and apply word identification strategies. The teacher regulates the amount of material to be read at one time, observes students as they read, and then moderates the discussion that occurs at stopping points when students use what they've read to evaluate their predictions and modify or formulate new ones if necessary.

The fourth step:
The students have made predictions and set purposes for reading. After reading they discuss the validity of their predictions, using information from the text and their prior knowledge to provide support. In the discussion, they further develop and refine purposes for reading. They may choose to stay with their original predictions or they may find that these predictions need to be redefined. The process of predicting, reading, and then proving their predictions is part of the ongoing process of developing comprehension. The group process allows students to learn from each other as they discuss ideas about the text. Students may also recognize the need for other source material as they gain additional information about concepts in the text.

The fifth step:
Students may become involved in a variety of activities after they have read the material. They may discuss the text, seek additional information from other sources about the content of the text, develop additional knowledge about text concepts, become involved in writing activities that are "spin offs" from text information, add to their knowledge of vocabulary, and/or sharpen specific aspects of word identification strategies. These activities tend to be mutually determined through discussion with the teacher.

Stauffer states:

> It should be evident at once that this DR-TA plan is not a process standing alone, to be used only in directing the reading of material. . . . Its doctrines are fundamental to problem solving, abstracting and analyzing information, propaganda analysis, and similar frequently occurring activities in which reading serves as an aid in the lives of children as well as adults in their search for truth and beauty (1969, p. 42).

There are some differences in how the DR-TA works when using content material or expository text, such as found in science and social studies materials. Students normally are directed to take a quick survey of section headings, captions under pictures, charts and graphs, and so forth. The teacher then asks them to speculate about what they expect to find developed or expanded upon in the material and why they think so and what they already know about these concept-oriented issues. The process continues much the same as it does with literature or basal stories, except that stopping points for discussion tend to be placed at the end of text sections.

DR-TA As a Problem-Solving Process

A great deal of the power of DR-TAs derives from the cooperative problem-solving environment that is established. Smith (1975) outlines four steps in learning and problem-solving:

(1) *The generation of a hypothesis*

(2) a *test* of the hypothesis . . . in order to obtain feedback,

(3) *feedback*, which provides new information against which the predicted consequence of the original hypothesis can be compared, and

(4) *acceptance or rejection of the hypothesis.* (p. 228)

The learning and problem-solving steps described by Smith are embedded in the DR-TA. Problem-solving patterns are identifiable and discernible throughout DR-TAs (Davidson, Padak, & Wilkerson, 1986). In literature, science, and social studies lessons that were investigated, students shared the cognitive responsibilities with the teacher. They generated hypotheses or predictions, they then read the material in order to test the validity of the predictions, they used the "new" information to compare the predicted consequence of their original hypotheses, and finally they accepted or rejected their original hypotheses. If their original hypotheses were rejected, they then formulated new hypotheses or modified their original ones, and the cyclical process continued. The students were actively involved in the process during the time of the investigation, and one day later a majority of the students were still involved in thinking that represented problem-solving (Davidson, 1985; Wilkerson, 1984). They tied new information with "old" through the predict, read, and prove process, thus showing the cyclical pattern of problem-solving throughout the lessons.

The problem-solving process moves from divergent thinking to convergent thinking in terms of plot in literature passages, **but thinking may not converge in terms of students' personal interpretations**, which is as it should be. The students begin the process of generating predictions with a limited amount of information about the text known to them but with all their prior knowledge and experiences as valuable resources. Intellectual creativity is at a high level as students explore all possibilities in forming

4

their predictions. Intellectual risk-taking is also exceptionally high as students grow increasingly aware that there is no one right answer, that they're treating chunks of information as clues which need to be carefully studied and considered. As the process continues and more information becomes known to them, their predictions converge towards the outcome (See Figure 1).

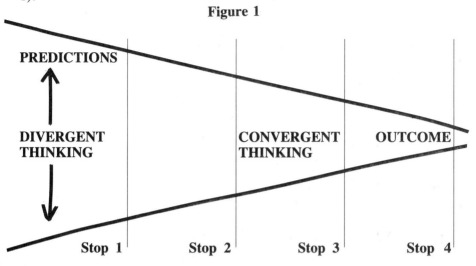

Figure 1

PROBLEM-SOLVING:
DIVERGENT TO CONVERGENT THINKING
DURING UNFOLDING STORY

During the cyclical process of predict, read, and prove, students in the group interact together in testing predictions and weighing evidence. As they evaluate their own thinking and that of their peers they say things like: "I don't think you're right about that because..." or "You might be right, but what about...?" "I don't think that (person in story) is going to matter in the ending. He's not really a major character so far..." is heard right along with "I think you're right because..." and "Well, what about...that (student in group) talked about? I didn't think of that and it could happen!" As Stauffer (1969) has written so eloquently, "What is most astonishing about all this is the integrity with which the reader operates. He is out to seek the truth and this is his dedication (p 44)."

Differences Between a DR-TA and a DRA

The Directed Reading Activity (Betts,1957; Chall,1967), commonly referred to as a DRA, is a traditional or "business as usual" means of reading and

5

discussing text. For many teachers this is probably because the DRA is recommended in many teachers' manuals in both basals and content text. The DRA includes the following steps:

I. **Vocabulary or Preteaching "New" Words:**
    Teacher writes each word on the chalkboard, usually in context, and the stresses the meaning of the word, along with necessary word identification strategies. Some of the current basal programs included use of workbook pages in the prereading phase.

II. **Motivation or Preparation for Reading:**
    Teacher tells students something about the story to be read that will spark students' interest in reading. Some of the current basals suggest a prediction question; others suggest asking a question that will be answered in reading.

III. **Silent Reading:**
    Students read to stopping point identified by teacher.

IV. **Comprehension Assessment:**
    Teacher asks questions that students can answer if they read the material. Oral rereading may be included; it focuses on skimming skills and locating specific information. Discussion may follow when the story has been completely read.

V. **Extending Skills:**
    Teacher assigns specific workbook pages to be completed by students.

In science and social studies materials, the manual suggestions for a DRA are similar to the above, except that most teachers see themselves in the role of the "teacher as a giver of information" (Davidson, Padak, and Wilkerson, 1986c) who adds additional information in the discussions. The pattern of read, discuss, and give information tends to continue throughout the lesson. Step V, Extending Skills, tends to focus on vocabulary activities and answering questions that are found at the end of sections and chapters of the content texts.

The difference between a DR-TA and the DRA is most obvious when we compare the two procedures step by step. Both the DR-TA and the DRA are designed for group instruction purported to increase students' comprehension, concept learning, and critical reading skills. Although differences between the instructional frameworks appear to be subtle, they are, in fact, substantial differences in focus. The focus of students' cognitive attention

6

differs which impacts the entire process of comprehension development. We'll begin by examining those differences in the two procedures when used with literature passages and basal reader stories.

The DRA begins by having the teacher preteach "new" words. New words are those which are appearing for the first time in the basal or ones that publishers think might be unfamiliar to students. In one current basal series, the words are to be printed in isolation on cards which are sent home to be practiced before the reading takes place. Usually the teacher writes the word on the chalkboard in a sentence. The students then read the sentence that contains the word. As all teachers know from experience, many of the students in the group already know the words. These students are not learning anything. Some students may know the "new" words, but they have difficulties with other words in the sentences, so the effectiveness of this strategy is questionable for them, too. Students who are wholly unfamiliar with the words are *not* going to learn them by seeing them in sentences written on the board. This part of the activity obviously doesn't lend itself to meeting the needs of any of the students in the group.

This step is omitted at the beginning of a DR-TA in literature or basal stories; instead, instruction in word identification strategies is provided by the teacher **following** the reading, when it is possible for the teacher to differentiate instruction for specific students in the group or, in some cases, for small groups of students in the class. It's frequently unnecessary to teach word identification to the students following reading, because students seem to work out word identification problems themselves. During the reading in a DR-TA, students are encouraged to put into practice what they have learned about word identification. They are urged to use the following steps that provide a functional system for word identification.

When you come to a word you don't know:
1. Skip the word and read to the end of the sentence.
2. Then go back to the unknown word.
3. Ask yourself, "What word would make sense in the sentence?"
4. If you can figure it out, then keep on reading.
5. If you can't figure it out, ask the teacher for help.

This functional system for word identification calls into play all the cueing systems used in identifying unknown words: pragmatic cues that narrow down the meaning possibilities, semantic (meaning) cues, syntactic (grammar) cues, and graphophonic (graphic similarities and phonics) cues. In the more traditional instruction these cues are frequently taught in isolation; for example, on one day a lesson on use of context or meaning cues and on the next day, phonics cues. The assumption is that students can integrate these strategies into a functional system. However, experience shows that many students need to be assisted in integrating the parts into the whole functional system. We remember very well a fifth-grade student who had been referred for diagnosis because she had difficulties in word identificaton. When she was assisted in applying the strategy described above, she was able successfully to put it to work as she read several pages of material. Flushed with success and undone by her own frustration at not having learned such a strategy before, she burst into tears and exclaimed, "Is this what you do! Why didn't anyone ever teach me about it until now!"

The second step in the DRA involves preparation for reading. In the DRA, the teacher starts off by talking about enough of the story to motivate students to read. Questions are then raised by the teacher. Students are to find answers to these questions when they read. The teacher obviously sets the purpose for reading in a DRA. In contrast, *the students set purposes for reading in a DR-TA*. The teacher asks two major questions after giving students some clues (the title of the story, or the first section of the story, or an illustration, etc.): *"What do you think will happen?"* coupled with *"Why do you think so?"* These two questions cause students to generate predictions and provide support for these predictions. Who sets the purpose in a DR-TA? The students do—their purpose for reading is to confirm their predictions. They have a need to know and read to find answers to questions they individually, and as a group, have generated through predictions. Providing support for their predictions causes them to draw upon their own personal experiences and information they've gleaned from the material they've read.

The hallmark of a critical reader is the ability to establish a purpose for reading (Stauffer, 1969). Who gets all the practice in setting purposes in a DRA? The teacher does. Who gets the practice in a DR-TA? The students do. On one hand, in a DRA, the teacher is doing more of the cognitive work, and on the other hand, in a DR-TA, the students are cognitively involved in setting their own purposes. The teacher and the students expend more time, effort, and talk in setting purposes.

In the silent reading step in the DRA, the students read to answer the questions that have been raised by the teacher. They do what they have been asked to do. They are reading, then, to answer someone else's questions. In our studies (Davidson, Padak, & Wilkerson; see Chapter V) we found, when we interviewed students the day following DRA lessons, that students were thinking about answers to the teachers' questions, or about not getting in trouble, or bits of the text that they were unable to piece together. During the DR-TA, students read to find out if their individual and group predictions (that function as purposes) are accurate, and if not, why not. They then think how the predictions might be reshaped. They are intellectually involved—thinking.

The next step in the DRA concerns comprehension development. The teacher asks questions following reading. *The task is one of assessment rather than development of student comprehension* (Durkin, 1978-79). The questions tend to demand "one correct answer" and many of the questions are factual in nature, representing thinking that does not go beyond the literal level of thinking. The teacher calls on individual students, following a pattern that involves asking a question, calling on a student who bids for a turn by raising a hand, and judging the students' responses as correct or incorrect. If the response is incorrect the teacher calls on another student until a correct response is received. If the response is correct then the correctness is acknowledged by the teacher who then asks another question.

In contrast, during the DR-TA, the students evaluate individual and group predictions after reading. Their discussion is a process of comprehension development. During initial experiences with DR-TA, the teacher may need to start off the discussion by asking the group if any of their predictions were accurate or partially accurate, and if so, how they know or how they can prove it. Students generally provide only that portion of the sentence or material that supports their points, tying in prior knowledge to evaluate and expand upon what they are reading. Sometimes they do this by recall, sometimes by reading a portion that provides the proof. Their reading is generally fluent because *they have a need for* effectively communicating that portion to others. Students also tend to have little difficulty locating specific pieces of information. Comprehension development is ongoing as the cyclical process of purpose setting through predictions continues: students use prior knowledge with the text being read to make additional predictions and set further purposes for reading.

These practices differ sharply from the oral rereading that takes place in a DRA, where the teacher asks, "Who can find the section to the story that describes....?" Again, the teacher using a DRA has set the purpose for the students. And, once again, the students do what they're instructed to do by the teacher. However, additional factors that occur in this practice in DRAs create a pedagogically unsound situation. For example, in every group there is a student who is more rapid at skimming than others. This student raises a hand to let the teacher know that the information has been located. Does the teacher call on this student to read the portion of text? No. The teacher waits for other or all of the students to complete the task. So, the skilled student(s) sit and wait, their arms waving listlessly in the air. The slowest student in the group is in agony—the longer the teacher waits, the more agonized the student becomes. The other students look on with pity, or sometimes derision. Finally, the teacher calls on one of the students to read. Oral rereading may be stilted, lack fluency, and tend to sound painful. If

9

the teacher does call on one student to read the text portion, the attention of the others wanders from the text. The overall group experience in a DRA is not conducive to a wholesome, successful learning experience.

A comparison of the two procedures shows that, during the DRA, the teacher sets purposes, assesses comprehension, and the students tend to find answers for questions asked by the teacher. During the DR-TA, students are actively involved in the ongoing process of problem solving: making predictions, reading a portion of material, and checking their predictions for accuracy, and then either rejecting their predictions and generating new ones or refining and reformulating their original predictions based on new information.

The last step in a DRA, Extending Skills, usually translates doing workbook pages. While there are some teachers who selectively use workbook pages to extend skills for some students, too often workbook pages are simply assigned to children to "do." The last step in a DR-TA provides the teacher with the opportunity to differentiate skills instruction for students, ranging from further discussion and analysis of the story or discussion of ways predictions might be improved, to small group or one-on-one instruction in specific skills identified by the teacher through observation while students were engaged in reading and discussion.

Learning As a Social Process: The Necessity for an Open Communication Structure for Discussion

Communication in a DR-TA is described as an open communication network in that each member of the group may communicate with anyone else in the group. The teacher moderates or serves as an "intellectual agitator" (Stauffer, 1980) of the group. The group, however, operates democratically; members interact with one another in setting purposes and goals by making predictions. Group members communicate freely with other members of the group, including the teacher.

We've known for a long time that learning is a social process. Students develop intellectually from the process of interacting socially with others in their lives (Vygotsky, 1962). The open communication pattern in DR-TAs permits students to interact freely with one another. Research has long supported such group communication (Bales, 1950; Bavelas, 1950; Leavitt, 1958) and suggested that groups that function this way are capable of task-centeredness, a sense of responsibility, and enhanced motivation (Taba, 1962). An instructional group in which students learn from one another tends to extend the scope of the learning (Davidson, 1978) and the process of expanding upon and refining new content leads to new learning strategies (Vygotsky, 1962; Berry, 1985).

As students interact with one another in the process of generating predictions and examining information to prove and disprove these predictions, the process is one of individual and group inquiry.

> "... the questions that the students themselves develop in an atmosphere of freedom, of natural and unbridled curiosity whereby they are encouraged to speculate and to investigate curiously the ramifications and the intent of the ideas which come to them through their reading. This ..., of course, is the inquiry process at work."
>
> (Courtney, 1968, p.35)

Members of a DR-TA group are actively involved and task-oriented. Human curiosity being what it is, students who commit themselves by making predictions have a natural tendency to want to find out if their predictions are accurate. Voicing their predictions, and reasons for those predictions, to their peer group causes an even stronger need to find out if their predictions are accurate. *There is no fear of failure* because the text has not been read in its entirety. Everybody, teachers and students, knows that predictions are educated guesses. The students are working with pieces of the story that they regard as clues or puzzle pieces, trying to see how those pieces might fit togeher as a whole.

The students work together in the group to predict outcomes and test their predictions. The teacher's role is to regulate the amount of material read during the lesson and to facilitate/moderate the group discussion. This role is one that has been described as "scaffolding," in that teachers "support children in achieving intended outcomes," and enter only to "assist or reciprocate or 'scaffold' the action" (Bruner, 1978, p 12). In other words, the teacher provides only that which is necessary for the student to go ahead. The process of scaffolding provides support to situations that allow students to interact and learn from their use of language (Scollon, 1976; Cazden, 1979). Note that the scaffolding process requires ongoing diagnostic judgement by the teacher who carefully listens to what students say and carefully observes them as they read.

The kinds of questions that teachers generally to ask in DR-TAs tend to be primarily prediction questions coupled with evaluative questions (Davidson, 1978). However, the teacher who is experienced in DR-TAs tends to ask a wide variety of additional questions and most of them are based on learners' responses. Figure 2 shows the relationship between teachers' questions and students' responses. The dynamics and interaction between the teacher and students, however, can cause some differences in the relationships between the teacher's questions and students' responses (Bloome,

11

TEACHERS' QUESTIONS AND STUDENTS' RESPONSES

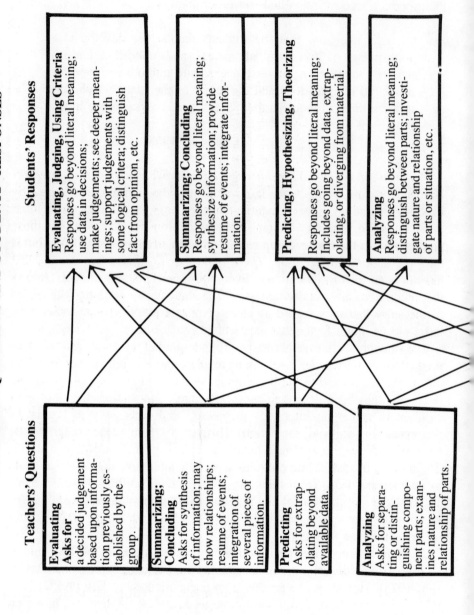

Figure 2

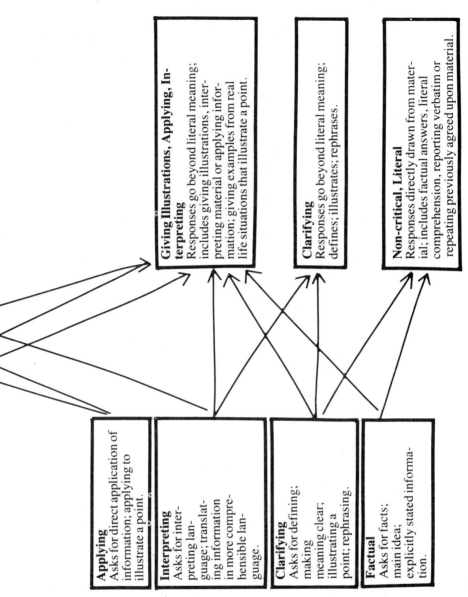

Giving Illustrations, Applying, Interpreting
Responses go beyond literal meaning; includes giving illustrations, interpreting material or applying information; giving examples from real life situations that illustrate a point.

Clarifying
Responses go beyond literal meaning; defines; illustrates; rephrases.

Non-critical, Literal
Responses directly drawn from material; includes factual answers, literal comprehension, reporting verbatim or repeating previously agreed upon material.

Applying
Asks for direct application of information; applying to illustrate a point.

Interpreting
Asks for interpreting language; translating information in more comprehensible language.

Clarifying
Asks for defining; making meaning clear; illustrating a point; rephrasing.

Factual
Asks for facts; main idea; explicitly stated information.

Note: Sometimes a factual question in a DR-TA will generate a response beyond the literal level and a higher level question in a DRA will generate a response that does not go beyond the literal level.

Adapted from the Ohio Scales (Wolf, King, & Huck, 1967).

1983; Davidson, Padak, & Wilkerson, 1986a). As the teacher and students interact, they also determine rules for the lesson, their roles, and values. As students become aware of the value on thinking in DR-TAs, they sometimes answer a factual question by making a critical response indicating thinking that goes beyond the literal level. Therefore, it is not always true that "you get what you ask for." The social nature of the lesson is the determining factor.

Figure 2 graphically shows the types of responses generally stimulated by specific questions. Most of the question types stimulate responses that represent critical thinking. Generally, factual questions do not. Asking additional questions during DR-TAs, based on students' responses, tends to provoke further thought and discussion from the students. By doing so, greater depth of thinking may be stimulated. In addition to the kinds of questions being asked, discussions can also be influenced by the behavior of the group. We know that communication structures can impact group behavior. Students' effectiveness as participating group members in reading instructional groups is affected by the communication structure. In an early study using the DR-TA, Petre (1969) reported findings showing students' effectiveness as participating group members in an open communication network that were similar in nature to findings from laboratory studies (Leavitt, 1958). Members can achieve higher levels of personal satisfaction in a group that functions with an open communication network with democratic leadership (Bavelas, 1950).

Abercrombie (1969), in her classic work *The Anatomy of Judgement,* discussed the impact of group interaction through discussion in problem solving. She related an anecdote about a student who, involved in group discussion, indicated that late in the discussion came the realization that there were many ways of looking at things that had not occurred to the student until they were contributed by others in the group.

> Discussion in a group does for thinking what testing on real objects does for seeing. We become aware of discrepancies between different people's interpretations of the same stimulus and are driven to weigh the evidence in favour of alternative interpretations. Certain areas of one's private world are compared and contrasted with other people's, and in seeing differences between them it becomes possible to modify our own world if we wish to. Instead of seeing our own mistakes by contrast with the statements of an unquestioned authority as in traditional pupil-teacher relationship, we see a variety of interpretations of the same stimulus pattern, and the usefulness of each must be tested in its own right. (p 75)

Classroom social patterns can be either diffuse or centralized (Guthrie, 1979). If the social pattern is described as diffuse, it means that each student is considered to be a friend by at least one other student. In a centralized pattern, at least one student, or a very small number of students, are identified as friends by all the other students; in other words, a few students are considered to be highly popular by the others. Guthrie reported findings from a study by Zeichner (1978) that showed that "students in diffuse classrooms achieved higher in reading than students in centralized classrooms" (p 501). Guthrie made the point that students' self-acceptance and diffuse classroom structures are related.

In DR-TAs, students feel a sense of self-worth when they work together with others in purpose-setting. The tyranny of "one right answer" is non-existent; the teacher accepts all responses either positively or in a neutral fashion. Instead, it is clear that the teacher and the students value thinking. It's fairly common to hear a student say to another, "I never thought of that!" or "(Student's name) turned out to be right about that!" Students also feel a sense of satisfaction and accomplishment in working together to problem-solve. Thus, students feel satisfied in working with group members and by knowing that others value their responses.

Open and Closed Communication Networks

Open and closed communication networks operate differently, impacting the social process of learning in different ways. The following diagrams may help in understanding the differences in the two communication networks.

Figure 3

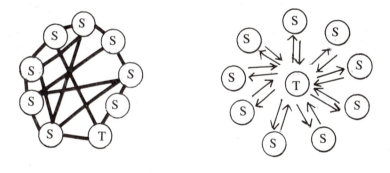

All-Channels-Open   **Closed Wheel**

The "all-channels-open" network (Bavelas, 1950) is similar to the network used in a DR-TA. This network allows everyone to communicate with other members of the group. In this network, no one must wait to be called upon by the teacher; instead, they enter into what can be regarded as a normal conversational flow of talk in that students speak when they wish to do so in the discussion. The teacher moderates the group discussion. In the DR-TA discussion, students formulate predictions, raise questions of one another, provide support for their reasoning, etc. They are not forced to communicate; they are free to talk, only if they choose to do so.

The "closed wheel" network (Bavelas, 1950) is similar to the communication network in a DRA. Restrictions are implicitly and explicitly imposed on group members in that they may only communicate with the "hub." The teacher serves as the hub in an instructional group. The interaction pattern that results is from teacher to student, student to teacher, teacher to student, and so on. Students may not communicate freely with others; they must wait to speak until they are called upon by the teacher. Even if students want to talk about someone else's comments, they have to work through the teacher.

Many teachers accentuate the differences in their roles in communication in the two procedures by changing where they sit with the groups. The following diagram illustrates these seating arrangements.

Figure 4

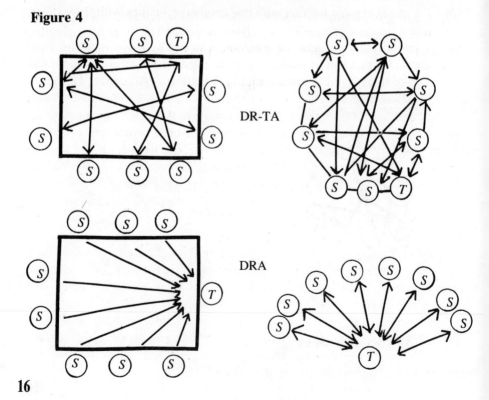

DR-TA

DRA

16

The teacher using a DRA usually stands or sits in a physically-dominating place, at the head of a table or the front of a group. The teacher in this position of authority can easily recognize students who wish to speak, judge the accuracy or "correctness" of their responses, and call upon or recognize others who are ready to participate. Students may or may not have eye contact with one another.

The teacher using a DR-TA usually sits *with* the group in a place where all students and the teacher can have eye contact and face-to-face interaction with one another. The teacher, as moderator of the group, takes a more democratic role in facilitating the discussion. The physical setting allows students maximum opportunity to talk across and with one another.

The exception may be the teacher in a content area who is using a piece of material that deals with concepts related to the content with an entire class. Obviously, the teacher needs to be in a position where it's possible to see all students. However, the facilitating role of the teacher does not change. A sensitive teacher will be careful not to interrupt when students are engaged in discussion of predictions and proof. Three criteria are important to remember in establishing communication networks of functional group discussion:

(1)   the discussants must present multiple points of view and be ready to change their minds [or at least accept another viewpoint] after hearing convincing counter arguments;

(2)   the students must interact with one another as well as with the teacher; and

(3)   a majority of the verbal interactions, especially those resulting from questions that solicit student opinion, must be longer than the typical two or three word phrases found in recitations. (Alverman, Dillon, & O'Brien, 1987, p 3.)

Directed Reading-Thinking Activities provide the communication structure, social and intellectual dynamics, and personal investment necessary for achieving the criteria for group discussion. The teacher should keep in mind that the role is one of facilitator involving, among other tasks, moderating the discussion and serving as intellectual agitator when needed.

Summary of the DR-TA Procedure

The DR-TA provides an on-going procedure throughout the material being read, as well as beyond the reading to spin-off activities and additional instruction. It should not be misinterpreted as a pre-reading activity as it has by some, for example Tierney & Cunningham (1980). The nature of problem solving ranges from divergent thinking at onset to convergent thinking at the conclusion of the reading. Figure 5 shows an illustration of the process of problem-solving and the types of teachers' questions and students' responses during and following the reading.

Figure 5
THE DR-TA PROCESS

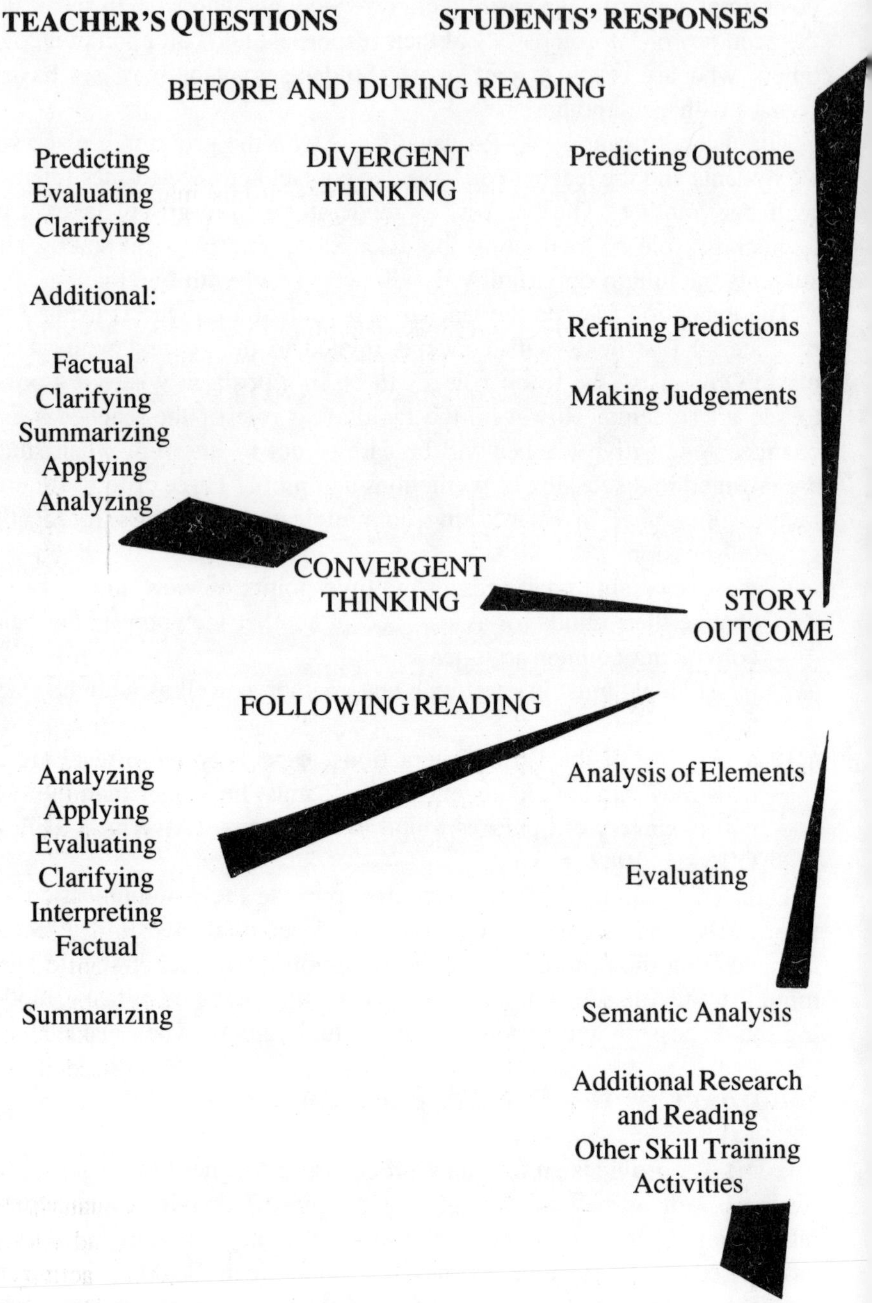

TEACHER'S QUESTIONS   **STUDENTS' RESPONSES**

BEFORE AND DURING READING

Predicting   DIVERGENT   Predicting Outcome
Evaluating   THINKING
Clarifying

Additional:
                                       Refining Predictions
Factual
Clarifying   Making Judgements
Summarizing
Applying
Analyzing

CONVERGENT
THINKING   STORY
                                       OUTCOME

FOLLOWING READING

Analyzing   Analysis of Elements
Applying
Evaluating
Clarifying   Evaluating
Interpreting
Factual

Summarizing   Semantic Analysis

                                       Additional Research
                                       and Reading
                                       Other Skill Training
                                       Activities

All in all, the teacher in DR-TAs shares with students the responsibility for the students' learning. The teacher is in a facilitative role in guiding students through the text. The teacher ensures that focus is on the students' purposes by making sure that the communication network is open. The basic DR-TA structure is learner-centered; the teacher makes certain throughout the evolving lesson that follow-up questions and comments are based on the reasoning and needs of the students in the discussion.

Discussions are dialectic in nature, or represent talk marked by dynamic tension. Manzo & Sherk (1978) describe the term dialectical as follows:

> a way of thinking characterized by a reciprocal interaction of information, precepts, and ideas struggling to be reconciled into clear patterns of thought. The tension between the ideas to be interconnected, or reconciled, is at the core of all sound learning situations. The purpose of education is to optimize these situations so that students can internalize and carry on a continuous dialectic within themselves, learning to explore, to be challenged by discrepancies, and yet to feel relatively fulfilled in the face of persisting ambiguities. (p 29)

Use of the DR-TA stimulates critical thinking from students. The group process is an essential ingredient. The open communication network allows the teacher to share the responsibility for the lesson with the students and they assume that shared responsibility at the onset of the lesson. Students, then, are active participants in the total process of comprehension attainment.

CHAPTER II

TEACHING DR-TAs

Organizing for instruction using a DR-TA is quite simple. It requires a text worthy of discussion and analysis, a group of students in a setting conducive to interaction, and a teacher prepared to facilitate discussion. This chapter describes how a DR-TA is implemented, and through use of excerpts from a transcript of a DR-TA in process, illustrates how the lesson evolves.

Text

Although some literature passages seem to be more naturally suited to the hypothesis generation and validation cycle of the DR-TA, the strategy is highly effective with passages that seem less readily "predictable." The primary consideration for selection of a literature passage for use with a DR-TA should be its inherent worthiness as good literature. The DR-TA, however, is by no means limited in use to literature. The strategy is highly effective for group reading and discussion of other content, such as social studies, science, and health texts, and supplementary contents like magazines and other materials. Texts selected for reading should be written at a level of difficulty which falls within the instructional range for the least competent reader in the group.

Students' Facilitation and the Importance of the Group

Group interaction is a critically important element of the DR-TA. The group is the primary vehicle for development of concepts as students interact with one another in making predictions, sharing ideas, brainstorming, making judgements, and learning from one another as they discuss the text.

Facilitating effective communication in the group requires consideration of the physical arrangements of group members as well as group size. The group should be arranged physically so that members can easily see and communicate with one another. The arrangement should facilitate the open communication network of student-to-student interaction. The teacher should not be placed in a position of primary focus. Circle arrangements, semi-circle arrangements, or rectangular arrangements all work well. The diagrams from Chapter 1, shown here, provide examples of effective group seating arrangements.

20

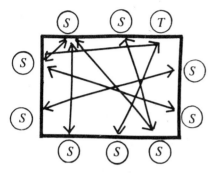 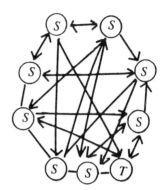

When determining group size it is important to remember that the group should be large enough to provide for an active sharing of information and ideas, while small enough to provide opportunity for participation of all group members and to encourage a feeling of group membership by all. DR-TAs may be implemented with fewer or greater numbers, but changes in the process and products of the discussion are inherent in very small or very large groups. Very small groups may restrict the discussion due to the smaller number of individuals available to share ideas, while very large groups may provide less opportunity for all individuals to verbally participate and more opportunity for disengagement from the group, with reduced cohesion and group purpose.

Teacher Facilitation

The DR-TA process evolves through the facilitation of the teacher. The process is a cycle of purpose setting through prediction, reading for those purposes—to confirm or refine the predictions made, discussing why predictions were confirmed, rejected, or refined in the reading, and setting further purposes through new or refined predictions. The elements of predict, read, and prove occur in a cycle throughout the reading and discussion of the text.

The teacher may begin the DR-TA by asking students to read the title of the text, to look at an illustration, or to read a portion of text. Students are then asked to predict what they expect the story to be about. A question such as, "From reading the title, what do you think this story will be about?" begins the process of the DR-TA. The teacher encourages students to extend their thinking, to provide justification, and to explain. Statements such as: "Why do you think so?"; "Talk about that a little more."; "More ideas?" are used by the teacher, after waiting for responses, to facilitate the purpose setting discussion. Students are not called on, but are encouraged to respond freely.

Student predictions, based on the limited information available in the title, illustration, or portion of text available to them will be diverse. This occurs because students bring forth whatever prior experience they have which seems relevant to the available information from the text in order to make predictions. These early predictions will be based on broad text-based and experience-based possibilities. As the text unfolds through reading and discussion, predictions will begin to converge as the possibilities, still built from a combination of prior experience and text, are more influenced and molded by information gleaned from the text. It's important to keep in mind that complete convergence will not occur; personal interpretations will vary.

When the momentum of making predictions based on the title seems to slow down, the teacher asks students to silently read to a predetermined stopping point in the text. Stopping points for reading and discussion are carefully predetermined before the lesson by the teacher. The teacher, in preparing for the lesson, reads the text to determine logical or natural stopping points for discussion. Text segments should be long enough to give students new information and provide material for prediction, and short enough to encourage interest, momentum in discussion, and a need to know more. Although stops within a text are determined before the lesson begins, the teacher must be sensitive to the flow of the discussion and be prepared to add or delete stops when it seems necessary in facilitating the discussion. Many teachers deliberately plan alternate stops and feel more free either to use them or to skip them, depending on whether or not students need more information for discussion.

After students have read a portion of text silently, discussion resumes. The teacher may facilitate by asking students whether their predictions were accurate. For example, "Were your predictions right?" Students accustomed to working with the DR-TA will spontaneously resume discussion by talking about the accuracy of their predictions. It is important that students justify their responses. Asking "Why?" facilitates this. The discussion of prior predictions will lead to the formulation of new predictions and purposes for reading. Variations of "What do you think will happen next?" and "Why do you think so?'' facilitate the new phase of purpose setting.

The DR-TA continues in a cycle of purpose setting, reading to confirm, refine, and generate new predictions (purposes), discussion to evaluate prior predictions based on new information read, and generation of new predictions. Text reading and discussion is followed by "Step 5" activities which are developed by the teacher to extend concepts and skills relevant to the text read. These activities may include vocabulary study, word identification strategy instruction, writing, further reading and inquiry study, drama, and art. The possibilities for Step 5 activities are limitless.

A DR-TA in Process: Literature

The transcript excerpts below are from a DR-TA in process (Davidson, 1987; Padak, 1987; Wilkerson, 1987). The group consists of eight eighth-grade students, four boys and four girls. The story they are reading, "All the Years of Her Life" concerns the relationship of an adolescent boy and his mother, revealed through an incident of the boy's stealing and the characters' reactions to the incident and to one another. The transcript provides a window on the evolving interaction of the students as they experience a DR-TA. The accompanying analysis is intended to make explicit the process of the DR-TA as it progresses and to analyze what is happening within the group and within the discussion. Teacher statements are printed in capital letters, student statements are printed in lower-case letters.

The first transcript excerpt is an example of an initial purpose setting/discussion episode in a DR-TA. The teacher uses the title of the story as an information source for students to predict from. She encourages them to explain and provide support for their predictions. The students provide support from the limited text available to them (the title) and their backgrounds of knowledge and experience. When the teacher judges that student purpose setting has been adequate to generate the need to read more of the text, she directs them to read a pre-determined portion of text.

WHAT DO YOU THINK THIS STORY'S GOING TO BE ABOUT?

The teacher has begun the discussion by having students set purposes by making predictions about the story from the title. Initial responses are short.

s: somebody's life

S: somebody

CAN YOU BUILD ON THAT?

She encourages more critical analysis by asking students to expand on their responses.

CAN YOU TELL ME SOME MORE ABOUT THAT?

s: it's her life
s: it'll be a diary about
her life

The expanded responses begin to extend beyond the literal information in the title.

s: yeah
s: could be a diary
WHAT ELSE DO YOU THINK?

The teacher is asking for more predictions and follows her request by asking students to expand on their responses.

S: Well, it was about a lady.

A LADY?
WHAT DID IT DO?
s: It was about her life.
DO YOU WANT TO MAKE ANY
PREDICTIONS ABOUT THAT
LADY?
CAN YOU TELL ME ANYTHING
ABOUT . . .
s: She's going to be older
s: She's old.
WHY DO YOU SAY THAT?

The teacher asks "why," one of the key questions in a DR-TA, to facilitate the student's analysis of the response and a sharing of that analysis with the group.

s: Well, it's a story about her life.
s: It says, "All the Years..."

In this response the student goes to the text and reads to provide support for the response.

s: yeah

s: so that means that...
s: So that means she's going to
be like older?
OK
WHAT ELSE WOULD YOU LIKE
TO GUESS THAT THIS MIGHT
BE ABOUT?

The teacher again asks students to consider possible predictions.

YOU SAID IT MIGHT INVOLVE
HER LIFE

UM, THE LIFE OF A LADY	*The teacher is asking students to extend their thinking*
WELL, WHAT KIND OF LIFE?	*and to elaborate.*
WHY DON'T YOU MAKE SOME GUESSES ABOUT THAT? s: Active. WHY DO YOU SAY THAT, JENNY? s: I don't know. s: Just guessing.	
s: Yeah.	*When the student indicates her inability to say "why" in regard to her prediction, the teacher accepts the*
A GUESS. O.K.	*student's guess but continues to encourage her to expand*
WHAT DO YOU MEAN BY AN ACTIVE LIFE? s: Well, sorta like...she had one baby and like that?	*upon it by asking her in another way.*
SOME OTHER PREDICTIONS?	*Here the teacher is asking for more predictions.*
s: Someone's problems. WHY DO YOU SAY THAT?	*She asks for reasoning for the prediction.*
s: I don't know. s: you can just tell by her life, and she...usually people have problems. OK. WHAT ELSE? s: Could be anything. s: uh huh	*The student draws on background knowledge in the response.* *Students are signaling by their responses that they need*
s: It doesn't specifically say.	*to have more information. The momentum of discussion is*
YEAH THAT'S WHY I WAS JUST SAYING FOR YOU TO GUESS.	*slowing.*

25

WE'RE JUST TRYING TO MAKE   *The teacher, sensitive to the*
SOME PREDICTIONS.   *flow of the discussion,*
                                    recognizes that the students
WE'RE NOT TRYING TO SAY FOR   *are ready to read for more*
SURE THAT IT'S GOING TO   *information. She reassures*
HAPPEN.   *them regarding the discussion*
WELL, WHY DON'T YOU GO AHEAD   *they have just had, and*
AND BEGIN TO READ THIS STORY.   *asks them to read a pre-*
                                    determined portion of the
BUT WHAT I WANT YOU TO DO   *text.*
WHEN YOU GET TO THE END OF
THIS FIRST PAGE

I WANT YOU TO STOP.

DON'T TURN THE PAGE.

STOP WHEN YOU GET TO THE END
OF THE PAGE.

(Students read silently.)

In the lesson's second segment, the teacher facilitates the discussion process by asking students if their predicitions were right, asking them to tell why, asking them what changes they would make to previous predictions, and encouraging them to make new predictions. This process of confirmation, rethinking, and generation of purposes for reading is the process of the DR-TA. It occurs with the teacher's facilitation as students gain experience with the strategy and it occurs as a spontaneous function of the reading/discussion cycle. The teacher's role is to facilitate the *process* of comprehension of the text. Teacher questions are rarely specific questions about the text. Instead, teacher questions are formulated to facilitate the students' purposes for reading and their discussion of the text in terms of those purposes. The teacher's "script" evolves from the students' discussion. Most simply stated, the teacher, in various ways, asks students what they think will happen next, why they think so, if they were right, and why. Other questions and statements enter where appropriate to encourage students to clarify, explain, extend, and further justify their responses.

WHO FEELS THEIR PREDICTION
WAS RIGHT?

YOU MADE SOME GUESSES ABOUT *The teacher initiates the*
WHAT THE STORY WAS GOING TO *discussion by asking students*
BE ABOUT. *to confirm their predictions.*
WHICH ONES WERE RIGHT?

s: Hers.

WHY WAS HERS RIGHT? *"Why" is used by the teacher*
to encourage a student to
s: 'Cause it was about a *extend the response and*
problem. *justify it. "Explain that" had the same*
purpose.

EXPLAIN THAT PLEASE.
s: Well, it was this boy has
a problem with stealing. *The teacher accepts the*
OK. WERE THERE SOME OTHER *response and asks for*
PREDICTIONS THAT WERE RIGHT? *further comments.*
WERE THERE SOME PREDICTIONS *The teacher asks*
THAT YOU'D LIKE TO CHANGE? *students to refine predictions.*
DID YOU MAKE A PREDICTION
YOU'D LIKE TO ALTER OR
REVISE IN ANY WAY?

s: It was a "him" and *Note the difference in this*
not a "her." *response and the one following*
the teacher's request for
WHAT DO YOU MEAN BY THAT? *explanation. Teacher questions*
such as this one, asking
s: It was a guy that *students to clarify or*
worked at the store *explain a response are very*
and not a lady. *important in facilitating the quality of*
WOULD YOU LIKE TO CHANGE *the discussion.*
YOUR PREDICTION THEN?
YOU'RE NOT SURE.
O.K.

ANY OTHER IDEAS ABOUT WHAT *These questions are*
THE STORY IS GOING TO BE *invitations to make new*
ABOUT? *predictions. Note that*
WOULD YOU LIKE TO ADD *the teacher does not ask*
SOMETHING? *questions about the story,*

DO YOU HAVE NEW IDEAS ABOUT
WHAT MIGHT HAPPEN IN THIS
STORY NOW THAT YOU'VE READ
A PAGE?

*but rather asks questions
to facilitate students'
validation of predictions
and further purpose setting.*

s: It might be bout how a
family gets…gets their
kid back straight.

*The student makes a
prediction that involves
what has been read in
the text, tied to his
own prior knowledge.*

WOULD YOU LIKE TO TALK SOME
MORE ABOUT THAT?

s: I don't know that much about it.

s: I just say it's about a family that helps
this…helps this little thief.

OK

ANY IDEAS ABOUT HOW THEY
MIGHT DO THAT?

*The teacher continues to
ask students to make predictions
and provide
support for them.*

s: Go to a counseling session.

UM HMM

ARE THERE ANY OTHER GUESSES
ABOUT WHAT MIGHT HAPPEN IN
THIS STORY?

s: They might give him a chance so he
can work out something so that he can
pay back probably for what he stole.

OK

WHAT ARE SOME OTHER
PREDICTIONS?

s: Maybe he should go to jail.

*This response represents a
judgement about the
character in the story and
is a sign that the student
is involved with the text
at a critical level.*

OK

s: If he'd go to jail, then after
he gets out of jail, how he'd
lead his life.

OK. DO YOU WANT TO MAKE ANY
GUESSES ABOUT HOW THAT
MIGHT BE?

The teacher asks the student to elaborate.

s: He could, like, be a bum or something.

OK. ANY OTHER GUESSES?

s: Well, if you…if you read
the…read the little note
at the top here, it talks
about how to understand Alfred's mother.

The student returns to the text to justify a prediction that is being considered.

s: It's probably about how his
mother copes with him.

AND HOW DO YOU THINK THAT
WILL BE?

The teacher asks the student to elaborate.

s: I think she'll get real mad.

s: Smack him or something.

OK. ANYONE ELSE?

TOM TOOK US BACK TO THE TITLE
AT THE BEGINNING. WHAT WE
TALKED ABOUT THERE.

The teacher, sensitive to the discussion, senses that the students need more information, but first gives

CAN YOU MAKE ANY PREDICTIONS
ABOUT THE TITLE NOW THAT
YOU'VE READ A LITTLE BIT MORE
ABOUT THE STORY?

students one more opportunity to predict.

WHO THAT "HER" IS?

The teacher asks students to interpret who "her" is.

s: Yeah

s: Has it up there.

WHERE DOES IT SAY IT?

The teacher requests that the student use the text to justify the response.

s: It says, "After you have
read the story which follows, see how you
would understand Alfred's mother."

I SEE.

LET'S GO ON TO THE NEXT PAGE.

The teacher instructs the students, telling them where the next stopping point is.

PLEASE READ THE ENTIRE PAGE,

BUT STOP WHEN YOU GET TO THE
END.
DON'T TURN THE PAGE.

(Students read silently.)

In the following excerpt from the lesson transcript, the process is the same. The students have read more of the text. They are then asked by the teacher to talk about the accuracy of the predictions they made before reading, to refine them, and to make new predictions. Students are asked to support their responses and to clarify and elaborate. However, *more student* facilitation of the discussion is evident in this part of the lesson as students question, extend, and justify the responses of other students. The student-to-student interaction typical of the open communication network of the DR-TA is evident in this excerpt. Also illustrated in this excerpt is the spontaneous support and elaboration of student responses without a request from the teacher to do so.

WHAT DO YOU THINK ABOUT THOSE PREDICTIONS THAT YOU MADE? *The teacher begins this portion of the lesson by asking students to confirm their predictions.*

s1: Someone said something about jail.

OK. WHAT ABOUT THAT? *She asks the student to elaborate.*

s1: He didn't go to jail.
He ended up calling his mom. *The student provides support from what was read.*

OK. DO YOU WANT TO STICK WITH THAT PREDICTION AS SOMETHING THAT MIGHT HAPPEN? DO YOU WANT TO CHANGE THAT? *The teacher asks for further clarification.*

s1: It might still happen. *The student responds without clarifying.*

YOU THINK SO. WHAT MAKES YOU THINK IT MIGHT STILL HAPPEN? *The teacher asks for clarification.*

s1: Well, now he doesn't seem to be changing. He just acts like it's no big thing, just doesn't want to get in trouble *The student elaborates, making judgements about the character's actions and motivation.*

OK

30

s2: It's also because in a way, his mother said, "Well, yeah. I think that's what you were supposed to do." Because the store manager said, you know, he was going to get a police officer. And mother said, "Yeah, that's what you should have done."

Another student elaborates on the first student's response.

SO WHAT DO YOU THINK ABOUT THAT? WHAT DOES THAT TELL YOU?

The teacher encourages more elaboration and interpretation.

s3: I think maybe there's…they still might go and have a police officer come in. See what he thinks of it.

A third student gives an opinion adding to the statements of the first two students.

OK. OTHER THOUGHTS ON THAT? (pause) DO YOU AGREE WITH THAT PREDICTION? (pause)

DISAGREE? (pause) UPDATE IT? (pause)

The teacher asks for more discussion on this prediction and receives no responses. This is a signal to the teacher that the discussion needs to move along to something else.

CHANGE IT? (pause) COME UP WITH ANOTHER IDEA OF YOUR OWN? (pause) WELL, WHAT DO YOU THINK WILL HAPPEN NEXT? (silence)

The teacher takes the cue and asks students to make new predictions.

s1: I don't think they're going to get a cop.

A student responds by disagreeing with the predictions of the previous three students.

NO? WHY NOT? s2: Why not?

The teacher and another student simultaneously ask for support of the statement.

1: I just don't think that. With the mother's attitude the way she came in, I think that it might have changed the owner's mind.

You know, with a mother
like this, maybe, you know,
the kid'll turn out OK.
IS THERE ANY SIGN OF THAT IN
THE STORY?
s2: Yeah.
s1: Well, he couldn't believe
the attitude that his mom
came in with. Maybe
that might change his opinion about her.
s3: I think that he's more
likely to get a cop if
she came in nice like that.
s4: That's what I'd do.
s2: Yeah, 'cause he thinks
that she's probably not
going to do anything to
him, or punish him for what he did.
s1: Or maybe the...
s2: He figures he'll go get
a cop and he'll straighten it out.
OK
s3: The store manager thinks
that the mother sort of
planned for him to take something.
OK. GO FURTHER WITH THAT.
WHAT ARE YOU THINKING OF?
s3: Well, like, she came in
real nice. It sounds
like, you know, "oh, well,
you know, he didn't mean
to steal anything."
And like when they get home, they'll say,
"how come you got caught?" or
something like that.
s2: Yeah. Keep stealing.
Like lipstick.
s4: Yeah, ladies' things.
s5: And he's taking things for home.
s3: And he's stealing things
for the home.
OK. WHAT DO THE REST OF YOU
THINK?
s6: Well, maybe why the store manager

The student supports the
prediction with an evaluation
of the characters.
The teacher asks for support
from the text. (Student chimes in.)

The student provides support
with an analysis of the
character's motivation.

A third student enters the
discussion and disagrees with
the first student's reasoning.
A fourth student gives input.
The second student provides
support for the opinion of
students 3 and 4.

Student 2 continues to
elaborate.

Student 3 makes a new
prediction by adding
information not found in the text.
The teacher asks for
elaboration.
The student elaborates
by predicting the
characters' actions
and motivations.

Three students agree with and elaborate
upon the student's response.

The student who made the original
statement in the sequence clarifies.
The teacher invites more participation.

32

let him off the hook is because he'll
punish himself enough.
The kid'll probably punish himself
enough that he doesn't need to go to jail.
TELL ME MORE ABOUT THAT.

A student responds and gives support for the response.

The teacher asks for more support and elaboration.

s6: Guilt.
s7: Yeah, the way he'll
feel about himself from now on.
And he probably won't do it again.
OK.
s3: Well, the kid's already
scared as it is.
s2: He should go to jail.

Two students respond with valuations of the character's predicted response.

A third student supports the two and elaborates.

Another student makes a judgment, disagreeing with the three students.

OK
s2: I say...
WHAT WERE YOU SAYING, TOM?
s3: I said the kid's real scared
as it is. I think, you
know, he'll sort of learn
from it. You know, he has
to have an experience to know
what it's like to get in big trouble.
OK. OTHER THOUGHTS?
WELL, TURN THE PAGE AND READ
THE FIRST COLUMN, BUT ONLY
TO THE END OF THE FIRST
COLUMN, AND THEN STOP.
IF YOU'RE GOING TO BE
TEMPTED TO GO ON, PUT
YOUR HAND OVER THAT RIGHT
HAND COLUMN SO THAT YOU
DON'T GO ON.

The teacher perceives that the student was interrupted before he finished, and moves in as facilitator to provide the opportunity for the student to elaborate.

At this point in the lesson, the students were still actively involved in making predictions. The level of involvement was high, and students were personally invested with a strong need to know whether their predictions were right. Rather than continue with purpose setting any longer, the teacher made the decision to go on with the reading, preserving the momentum in the discussion, ready for it to reemerge in the post-reading discussion.

Each transcript excerpt above reveals a high level of student involvement in reading and discussion. It is a student discussion which evolved from questions asked and answered by the participants. The teacher acted as a facilitator who asked questions designed to engage students in generating their own questions, in the form of predictions, and through discussion of those questions, analyzing the story and its characters as they were revealed to them through reading. The teacher gauged her involvement according to the support students needed. This is a good example of scaffolding at work.

Step 5 of the DR-TA in this lesson focused on further comprehension development through discussion. The teacher used the Group Mapping Activity (Davidson, 1982) to facilitate further critical analysis of the story.

The story used in the lesson in this transcript was simple in plot and complex in character. Answers to questions regarding action in the story which were generated in predictions could have been quite simply and literally answered. For example: "Whose life?" — "Alfred's mother's."; "Did they call the police?" — "No." However, the process of the DR-TA provided the impetus for students to become involved in the real substance of the story, the complexity of the character relationships.

A DR-TA in Process: Science

The interaction of students' prior knowledge with textual information is essential for learning new concepts. Learning occurs as students are able to relate new information and concepts to their existing understandings of the world. The Directed Reading-Thinking Activity provides a forum for students' drawing forth relevant prior knowledge to anticipate information and concepts in the text and to evaluate and integrate new concepts with existing knowledge. It provides the means for students to set purposes for reading which are meaningful to them, to create a readiness to interact with concepts presented in the text.

The transcript excerpts below are from a DR-TA in science (Davidson, Padak, & Wilkerson, 1986a). Eight students, with the teacher acting as facilitator, are reading and discussing a science textbook chapter about the light spectrum. The first transcript segment illustrates the students' brainstorming of prior knowledge as they anticipate the information the text will reveal. As students share information they expect to find, they become involved in the process of evaluating and analyzing the shared information. In doing so, their discussion shifts from information to concepts. Thus they begin the actual reading with some notions about relevant concepts, and with questions about the validity of their notions. Student purposes, a need to know, have been effectively set.

I'D LIKE FOR YOU TO BEGIN BY JUST READING THIS ACTIVITY IN THIS SECTION. THEN TELL ME WHAT YOU EXPECT TO FIND IN THIS PASSAGE. YOU KNOW IT'S ABOUT LIGHT AND COLOR AND SPECTRUMS. WHAT ELSE DO YOU EXPECT THAT YOU WILL FIND?

The teacher directs students to read a description of an activity designed to produce a sun's spectrum with a prism. The activity includes holding a thermometer in the spectrum produced, placing a flourite substance near the spectrum, and anticipating changes.

s: Heat.

WHY DO YOU SAY HEAT?

s: Well, some of the colors are cooler.

The student's response is based on prior knowledge which she judges will be relevant.

DO YOU KNOW WHICH ONES WILL BE COOLER?

The teacher encourages the student to extend the response.

s: I think the darker ones.

WHY DO YOU SAY THAT?

Teacher asks for justification.

s: They look cooler.

THEY LOOK COOLER? OKAY.

Teacher accepts response, recognizing that the student has, in fact, generated a question to be answered in reading the text.

WHAT ELSE? DO YOU AGREE OR DISAGREE?

The teacher encourages other students to analyze this hypothesis or generate a different one.

s: Well, I agree with her on infrared and ultraviolet. They are probably the the hottest colors you can get of the spectrum.

The student's response shows that he is evaluating the other student's response. Also, he uses specific vocabulary from his prior knowledge to extend the prediction.

ALL RIGHT. ANYBODY ELSE?

The teacher does not make a judgement about the validity of the predictions since that is the responsibility of the students as they read and discuss.

s: I think he is wrong.

A student disagrees.

WHY?

Teacher asks for justification.

s: Because whenever you melt

The student analyzes the prior

steel, steel always turns
red before it turns white. When
it turns white, it melts completely.

student's prediction and
explains in terms of his own
experience.

OKAY.
s: You can't see infrared.

As stated, the student's
response is a literal statement.

AND HOW WOULD THAT MAKE A
DIFFERENCE IN WHAT HE JUST
SAID?

The teacher assumes
that there is a connection with the
discussion and asks for explanation.

s: Well, he just said that
it turned red before it
turned white. And you
can't see white, it's
just a shade. Infrared
you can't see—which
would be just like sun-
light. You can't see
sunlight. So, I think it would be hotter.

In his extended response
the student disagrees with
the prior student's con-
clusion and explanation and
uses an illustration from his
prior knowledge which he feels
is relevant to ''prove'' his
point.

YOU THINK IT WOULD BE HOTTER?
OKAY.

ANYBODY ELSE?

WELL, LET ME GIVE YOU THIS
WHOLE FIRST PARAGRAPH. I
WANT YOU TO READ TO THE
BOTTOM OF THE PAGE AND THEN I
WANT YOU TO GO OVER ON YOUR
PAGE. IT WILL BE THE VERY TOP
PARAGRAPH. COVER UP
WHAT'S BELOW IT WITH YOUR
PAPER.
READ THAT FAR AND THEN STOP.

The teacher does not point out
the validity or lack of validity
of either student's
logic. She recognizes that both
students are thinking
critically and that they and
others in the group will read
to find clues to justify the
concepts they are hypothe-
sizing. She is consistent in
her role as a facilitator of
student discussion.

(Students read silently.)

In the process of making predictions about what they expected to find in the text the students shared and analyzed their prior knowledge, experience, and understanding of concepts and information which they judged to be relevant. This sharing, along with the evaluation and analyses of the concepts, allowed them to generate questions and to develop the need to have those questions answered. Their purpose as they began to read was to find the answers to questions they had asked through the discussion.

When students read the portion of the text they were directed to read, they read that infrared waves are invisible and that they are heat waves. Discussion, involving text ideas, students' previous ideas, and their reasoning abilities, showed that they discovered that infrared light is *not* one of the hottest colors because it is not a color. They also discovered that infrared waves are hot, since they are heat waves. The text supplied literal information. The discussion facilitated concept development and critical thinking.

Note that students made predictions that were wrong or far afield of the concept. Teachers usually want to tell students that their statements were wrong. However, during DR-TAs, the appropriate things to do is *nothing*— let the students work it out themselves! Students are capable of judging the accuracy of predictions; they don't need input from the teacher in order to do so.

The next transcript excerpt illustrates a subsequent purpose setting episode in the cyclical DR-TA in science. It differs somewhat from the purpose setting episodes in literature. In literature the hypothesis generation and refinement through reading and discussion is facilitated as a generative process throughout the story. The discussion in literature can build and converge toward a story resolution because the nature of ''story'' is a set of related incidents which build toward an end. In this science text and in many other content texts a concept or set of related concepts are introduced and explained. The text then moves to another concept or set of related concepts. Although the entire segment of text used in the science lesson dealt with aspects of light, it was organized in sections which were separate and did not provide a natural cohesion to facilitate predicting from one section to another. Therefore, after the cycle of predict-read-prove had been repeated a number of times to complete one related section of text, the teacher was faced with a section of text which shifted both topic and emphasis. She continued the DR-TA by introducing the new section of text in much the same way she had initially begun the lesson.

TAKE A LOOK AT THE NEXT PAGE   *A portion of text is made*
& READ THAT FIRST PARAGRAPH   *available to students to*
& GO NO FURTHER.   *provide a focus for predicting.*
(Students read silently.)

ALL RIGHT, NOW WHAT DO YOU THINK YOU'RE GOING TO GET INTO? WHAT ARE THEY SETTING YOU UP FOR ON THIS ONE?	*The teacher asks students to make predictions based on what they have read.*
s1: About which colors reflect.	
DO YOU KNOW, CAN YOU GIVE AN IDEA ON WHAT THOSE MIGHT BE? WHICH COLORS REFLECT? HAVE YOU GOT ANY IDEAS ON THAT?	*The teacher asks the student to extend her response.*
s2: I think it's darker colors.	*A second student, who apparently agrees with the prediction, extends the first student's response.*
DARKER COLORS?	
s2: They absorb more light than the lighter colors.	*The student explains his response. The response reflects a change from the first student's prediction.*
ALL RIGHT. WHAT ELSE?	
s3: How they're combined?	*A third student offers another prediction.*
TELL US ABOUT THAT.	
s3: How they're combined to make different colors and stuff like that.	*The extended response clarifies for the group.*
OKAY. DO YOU KNOW WHAT HAPPENS TO SOME OF THEM? ANYBODY ELSE?	*A request for more explanation is not responded to. The teacher makes the decision to provide the students with more text.*
READ THE NEXT PARAGRAPH. (Students read silently.)	
OKAY, WERE YOU RIGHT ABOUT ANYTHING ON THIS ONE?	*The teacher begins by asking students to confirm their predictions.*
s4: No.	
s2: No.	
WHY?	*She asks for justification.*
s2: Because like her shirt will only reflect red and her shirt will only reflect the pink, but all other colors are absorbed.	*The student explains a text concept to prove his prediction wrong.*
AND WHAT DID YOU SAY THIS	

38

SECTION WAS GOING TO BE
ABOUT?
s2: The reflection and the absorption—
what lights reflect and what lights absorb.
SO YOU REALLY WERE RIGHT
ON THAT.

s2: Kind of, but I was wrong *The student's analysis of her*
when I said how, you know, *rejection of her prediction*
which ones do, because all *reflects understanding of a*
of them do. *very difficult concept presented in the text.*
NOW WHAT MAKES THE *The teacher's request for*
DIFFERENCE ON WHAT YOU SEE? *clarification is posed to generate more*
analysis and discussion of the concept.

s3: It depends on what color *Another student reflects*
the object is. *understanding and shares information*
which will help clarify the concept for
others in the group.

IT DEPENDS ON WHAT COLOR THE *The teacher is asking students*
OBJECT IS AND WHAT ELSE? *to extend their responses.*
s2: What light it reflects. *More information is shared*
with the group by a student.

The lesson continued throughout in the same manner. In generating hypotheses about what they expected to read, students brainstormed prior knowledge about the concepts and shared that information with others in the group. As they read, they evaluated the assumptions they made prior to reading in light of new information gained from the text. The discussion provided a forum for working through the concepts they were developing. Students learned from each other as well as from the text, and did so as critical listeners and readers, evaluating in terms of what they expected. They were also able to tie or link together the relationships among the concepts.

In Step 5 of the DR-TA the teacher asked a question posed in the text, "What colors would you see in the United States flag if it were viewed under red light?" She asked them to apply the information they had just read. The discussion which evolved followed the same agree, disagree, support, and sharing of information focus evident in the reading discussion. The purpose of the Step 5 activity was further comprehension development through group problem solving and discussion.

A DR-TA in Process: Social Studies

A DR-TA, whatever the genre of the text, begins with student purpose setting through prediction. Usually the focus of the initial purpose setting is a sampling from the text such as a title, a few lines of text, a graph, or an illustration. The focus may, as in the lesson illustrated here, be facilitated before the text itself is read or viewed. A DR-TA in social studies may begin with the teacher facilitating students' exploration of a key concept of the text to provide a broad focus and to begin to create a mind set for the text. Due to the nature of the initial pre-reading discussion, students focus on the conceptual theme of the text to be read, tying it to prior concepts, and developing a readiness to discover the relevant prior knowledge they hold as they analyze subsequent text information to make predictions. The vehicle for the discussion is brainstorming, predicting, and analyzing. The discussion is carefully focused through the facilitation of the teacher.

The lesson proceeds in the cycle of prediction (purpose setting), purposeful reading (to confirm, reject, and refine predictions), and evaluation (through discussion and analysis of the ongoing prediction/purpose setting cycle). In the lesson illustrated below (Wilkerson, 1984), boldfaced subtitles in the text are used as a focus for predictions and as appropriate reading "stopping" points in the lesson. The subtitles appear in the text to introduce changing areas of focus within the overall focus of "reform." The teacher sets additional stopping points within these major sections for comprehension development through discussion. In the discussion, students analyze the text segment they are reading and refer to concepts discussed in preceding segments.

Throughout the reading and discussion, the predictions generated serve as student purposes for reading, creating a readiness for the interaction of concepts students have in their heads with the information presented in the text. The confirmation, rejection, and refinement of predictions after reading of text segments serve as a vehicle for students to add new knowledge and evaluate prior understandings and concepts inrelation to the concept being studied. The cyclical process of setting purposes for reading through predictions, reading to refine, reject, confirm and make new predictions, and interacting student-to-student to evaluate those predictions occurs throughout the lesson.

In the lesson transcript segment shown below, the teacher tells students that the chapter they are going to read is about "reform." Asking them what the term "reform" means, she begins the prediction process. Her facilitation of predictions in this beginning is subtle; what appears to be a request for a definition is in fact the impetus for students' brainstorming of prior concepts about the term. This brainstorming provides responses which represent predictions about the material to be read and which set the stage for purposeful reading of the introductory material in the chapter.

THE PASSAGE YOU ARE GOING TO READ IS ON REFORM. WHAT DO YOU KNOW ABOUT REFORM?

The teacher initiates the discussion by focusing on a word which labels the key concept of the passage.

WHAT DOES REFORM MEAN TO YOU? LET'S START THERE. DO YOU HAVE ANY IDEAS?

Asking students to define the word, she is helping them to set purposes for reading the first section of text.

s: To be reshaped.

TELL US ABOUT IT.

She chose to begin this way, rather than by having students read a title or text, because she judged the text required student purpose setting from the outset.

s: To have a different shape. Maybe, to like when you model with clay you give it a different structure.

ALL RIGHT. AND REFORM IN THAT INSTANCE WOULD MEAN TO RESHAPE THE WHOLE THING.

Accepting one response and explanation, she asks for other ideas. The message here is that there is not one right answer. Other definitions and explanations are needed to explore and develop the concept of "reform."

ANY OTHER WORDS YOU CAN THINK OF THAT MIGHT HAVE THE WORD REFORM IN THEM?

s: Change?

WHY DO YOU SAY CHANGE?

s: Change from something else to something, reform, like change your ways.

Students are sharing concepts they hold from prior knowledge about "reform."

IN OUR COUNTRY, WHEN OUR COUNTRY WAS SETTLED, WE GOT TO A PERIOD OF TIME WHEN PEOPLE WERE CONCERNED ABOUT THINGS IN OUR SOCIETY. AND THAT'S THE SECTION THAT

The teacher provides some background to help set the stage for students to read a portion of the text, keeping in mind their discussion of the concept of "reform." Note that she

YOU'RE GOING TO BE READING
ABOUT TODAY.
READ THE FIRST TWO
PARAGRAPHS AND NO FURTHER
AND THEN WE'LL TALK ABOUT
POSSIBLE REFORMS.

uses "changing" from the student's use of the word "change" for "reform." The two paragraphs students are directed to read contain further introductory material, which the teacher judges the students now are ready to read. Purposes for reading have been developed by students with the teacher's facilitation.

(Students read.)

OKAY. NOW WITH THAT THOUGHT
IN MIND, THE SECTION THAT YOU
ARE GOING TO READ TODAY IS
ABOUT A WOMAN NAMED
DOROTHEA DIX. THE SECTION
SAYS, "*Dorothea Dix and the Mentally Ill.*" WHAT DO YOU SUPPOSE SHE
DID? WHAT DO YOU THINK YOU
ARE GOING TO READ ABOUT?

The teacher directs students' attention to the first bold faced subtitle in the social studies text chapter.

She asks students to make predictions.

s4: About her helping people.

WHY DO YOU THINK SO?

s4: Cause it says the mentally
ill.

ALL RIGHT. I THINK THAT'S A
GOOD POSSIBILITY. WHAT'S
ANOTHER ONE?
s3: Probably because it said
something about reform or
helping or something should
be reformed.

The response reflects understanding of one purpose of "reform." It also reflects effective purpose setting. The student's prediction is based on an interaction of the limited text information, the pre-reading discussion, and her existing concept of "reform." Although the teacher's request was for another prediction, a second student chose to give more explanation for the first student's prediction. This reflects a high level of involvement and investment in the discussion.

WHAT KINDS OF REFORM DO YOU
THINK NEEDED TO BE MADE?

The teacher asks for more explanation, encouraging students to use background

42

*knowledge to anticipate information
they are about to read.*

s3: Helping them get better.
ALL RIGHT. THAT'S ONE
POSSIBILITY. WHAT ELSE?
s5: Like if some people, like
if she helped people that
couldn't walk try to make
them walk that would be a change.
NOW RELATE THAT TO THE
MENTALLY ILL. WHAT SORTS OF
CHANGES COULD SHE ACHIEVE
THERE?

*The student's prediction is
based on the notion of
"reform."*

*The teacher does not tell the
student that he is off-track,
but encourages him to apply his concept
of reform to the mentally ill. The teacher
is patient. She knows the student is off-
track and wants him to work it out.*

s5: If someone hadn't walked
in a long time and she had
been working with them for
a few years maybe they could
walk better.

*Although the student's extended
response still does not
make application to the
mentally ill, the teacher accepts the
prediction,
knowing that the student will*

ALL RIGHT. ARE THERE ANY
OTHER POSSIBILITIES.

*have the opportunity through reading to
reject his own hypothesis and clarify
the concept.*

s1: Yeah. Because some of the
mentally ill are slower, she
could take more time so they
may be a few grades down
from the average person, but
still they'd be able to learn a lot of things.
I DON'T WANT TO PUT WORDS IN
YOUR MOUTH ON THIS, BUT
YOU'RE SAYING THEY MIGHT BE
SLOWER IN TERMS OF THEIR
INTELLIGENCE?
s1: Umhum.
WHAT OTHER POSSIBILITIES
WOULD THERE BE?

*Another student makes a different
prediction based on her
knowledge of the mentally ill
and what changes might be
appropriate.*

*The teacher clarifies in the
form of a question to the
student.*

The student agrees.

s6: They help reform on the attitudes so they think better of themselves so they don't put themselves down so much.
ALL RIGHT. ANYTHING ELSE?

Still another student predicts. In doing so, the student makes a judgement about the self-concept of people who are mentally ill.

WELL, LET'S SEE IF YOU'RE RIGHT. READ THAT SECTION. IT GOES DOWN FOR SEVERAL PARAGRAPHS AND IT STOPS AT THE TOP OF THE RIGHT HAND COLUMN.

(Students read.)

WHEN YOU'RE FINISHED JUST SIT BACK AND I'LL KNOW THAT YOU'RE THROUGH.

(This instruction is a management technique used by the teacher to help her know when most students are ready to begin the discussion.)

WERE YOU RIGHT ABOUT ANYTHING?
WHAT WERE YOU RIGHT ABOUT?

The post-reading discussion begins with a request for students to evaluate their predictions, based on what they have read.

s3: She was trying to help them.
IN WHAT WAY?
s3: Trying to reform them.
DID YOU FIND OUT ANYTHING ELSE THAT YOU WERE RIGHT ABOUT, THAT YOU PREDICTED?
s5: They don't help. Cause, in the last paragraph it says that all they needed was decent care, love, and understanding.

Answers to many questions generated by students in their predictions were not answered in the segment of text. Rather, it provided more background and the need for more information from which to predict.

ALL RIGHT. THIS NEXT SECTION IS CALLED, ''The Dix Report Brought Action.'' WHAT DO YOU EXPECT

The teacher directs students to make predictions about the next text segment, directing

44

THAT YOU WILL FIND OUT IN THIS PARTICULAR SECTION? YOU DON'T HAVE TO RAISE YOUR HANDS.

their attention to the bold-faced subtitle. She is aware that the text they have just read has given them information to use in extending and refining their earlier predictions. The DR-TA process of "feed forward, feed back" involves students in evaluating what they have just read as they interpret how to make use of the information in forming hypotheses about the next section.

s7: What people did and what they thought of her when they found out what she was doing. They probably thought, why would she want to help them?

The student's prediction extends beyond the actions of reform and into the area of human response to reform efforts.

WHAT DO YOU THINK WOULD HAPPEN, MARK?

The teacher is asking for an extension of the student's evaluative prediction.

s7: Well, people might think she was crazy and they would try to hurt her and stuff and try to stop her from doing this.

The students response is built on his existing knowledge of human response, which he relates to the issue of reform.

WHY DO YOU THINK THEY'D THINK SHE WAS CRAZY?

The teacher encourages him to analyze further his response.

s7: Well, they'd think, why would she want to do that, why would she want to help them?

s1: Because it was something they couldn't understand.

A different student explains why.

WHY NOT?

s1: Because they were brought up that way and to believe things like that.

She extends her explanation.

UMHMM.

s1: It was just something, if someone was crazy you just ignored them sort of like.

She is using her own interpretation of the facts she read in the last section to further clarify her response.

HOW ELSE DO YOU THINK THAT

The teacher asks for more

HER REPORT MIGHT BRING SOME
ACTION OR SOME CHANGE?

predictions.

s5: Like if there was, like it
said, there was a person
chained to the floor, they
might think that that person
is real dangerous and not
want her to go near him.
And then take actions to keep her away.

*This student also uses
facts from the text about
actions toward the mentally
ill to make assumptions
about attitudes and
motivations.*

s3: Some people might want to
help her too.

*The student suggests the
possibility of more than one reaction.*

IN WHAT RESPECT?

Teacher asks for more information.

s3: Try to help her while she's helping
the people.

s5: Help find places for them to
stay instead of in basements
of houses and that.

*The students are interacting freely,
exploring the concept
from a values' perspective,
using facts and information
from the text to examine critically the
issues they are*

s7: But some people might get
mad at that. At her trying to find other
places for them because it would
cost them money.

reading about and discussing.

OKAY. ANY OTHER THOUGHTS
ON THIS?

*The teacher is facilitating the continuation
of the discussion.*

s1: They might get mad at her
because they might be ashamed of a
person being related to them.

Another student joins in.

ANY OTHER THINGS THAT
COME TO MIND ABOUT THIS?

s5: Some people, like if
they're related to one
of the people who are sick,
they could take action to
help find somewhere else
and help Dorothea Dix to
help try and change the
life of the people.

*The student is problem
solving as he makes his
prediction. The prediction
contains elements
from the text and from
the discussion. He has
developed a scenerio from
the information available to him which*

46

moves him from the literal facts of the
text, to values judgements about the
situations, and to the development
of solutions.

ANYBODY ELSE?
WELL, LET'S LET YOU READ THIS
SECTION. STOP WHEN IT GETS TO
PRISON REFORM. READ TO SEE IF
YOU'RE RIGHT.

(Students read.)

WELL, WHAT WERE YOU RIGHT
ABOUT?

The teacher begins by asking for
discussion in relation to students'
predictions.

s3: They did try to help her
instead of, you know,
thinking that she was
crazy because she wanted
these people.
s1: And they found a place for
them to go.

Students found confirmation
for their predictions about
people's attitudes through
factual information in the to help
text about actions taken by the people.
Their discussion prior to reading
took them beyond the factual scope of
the text, allowing

s5: The people who heard, who
had seen her report helped
pay the money to enlarge the
hospital for them to stay and get the
treatment that they needed.

them to use the text information
to develop concepts
that extend beyond.

ANYTHING ELSE?
THIS NEXT PART IS ON PRISON
REFORM. NOW, YOU'VE TALKED
ABOUT MENTALLY ILL, LET'S
THINK ABOUT WHAT SORTS OF
CHANGES YOU THINK THERE NEED
TO BE MADE IN PRISONS. WHAT
WILL YOU PREDICT?

Once again, the focus of the
text, within the broader focus
of reform, shifts. The
teacher uses the bold faced
text subheading to initiate
purpose setting for the new
section of text.

The remainder of the DR-TA in social studies proceeded in much the same manner. The focus in the lesson was on the development of concepts and generalizations. Students read factual information in their text, and due to the nature of the DR-TA lesson framework, discussed the concept of reform from the perspective of motivations, values, and human response. Step 5 in the DR-TA involved a discussion of the end of the chapter questions. Questions concerned identifying specific actions which reformers took to create change. Students in the group quickly responded to the questions and noted that their discussion had gone well beyond the questions addressed in the text. As in the science lesson, students were able to tie concepts together.

In Summary

The DR-TA cycle of predict, read, and prove must not be mistaken for a cycle of "I was right; you were wrong; let's try again." It is a creative process. Through a process of evaluation of predictions in terms of what has been read, students create, develop, and discover the substance of the text. What they create is based on what they have read, on their prior experience, and on their evaluation of the actions, characters, facts and information in the text. What they create is not static. It is viable and changes as the discussion evolves and as more information is available to students through reading.

The sequence of steps in the Directed Reading-Thinking Activity is consistent, whatever the type of text being read and discussed. Students set purposes for reading by generating predictions. They engage in purposeful reading to test their predictions. They interact in meaningful discussion, developing comprehension as they analyze their prior hypotheses and generate new predictions. The sequence is cyclical, culminating in an activity or discussion designed to provide an extension to the text. The teacher serves as facilitator of the group discussion in which students are active participants in the development of comprehension. Students begin by making divergent predictions about broad possibilities, working with limited text information. Through group discussion the process of confirmation, rejection, refinement, and generation of predictions merges as students critically analyze the text. In literature, predictions about explicit elements become more convergent as students move toward story resolution and comprehension of the text through the reading/discussion cycle. In content text such as science and social studies, students' predictions converge as they refine their understanding of a conceptual focus, and expand as they apply that focus to their world experience. The product of the process of the DR-TA is purposeful, critical reading and discussion. The critical elements in that process are the text, open communication, and interaction of the teacher and the students as they work together to attain meaning.

CHAPTER III

POINTERS AND PROBLEMS

Most teachers find that expertise in the use of DR-TAs begins to develop from repeated experiences with the procedure. Teachers who are experienced in the use of DR-TAs also say that every time they use the procedure they learn something about the teaching-learning process that they didn't know before. Some discussion on teaching tips and how to avoid possible problems may provide some additional insights about the procedure, as well as help teachers refine and develop their skills in its use.

Teacher Preparation Is a "Must"

Preparing ahead of time pays off by allowing the teacher to concentrate more on what's happening in the lesson. Preparation involves two basic types: selection and preparation of material along with planning to ensure that the physical set up facilitates participation.

The material needs to be carefully selected. Will the material be interesting to the students? Is it well written? For fiction, is there a reasonable outcome? Reading the material thoroughly beforehand provides an opportunity to anticipate places where students may have difficulty in understanding meaning or concepts, and make decisions about stopping points and alternate stopping points for discussion. Alternative stopping points should always be determined. Sometimes students have difficulty making predictions because they don't have enough information; sometimes students' interests are so high that a number of stopping points can be skipped. By predetermining alternate stopping points, the teacher is free to use them when students need more information in order to form predictions or free to skip them when students' interests are high. A rule of thumb to follow in determining stopping points is that when students are relatively inexperienced with the procedure, there may need to be a few more stopping points early in the reading. Accordingly, depending upon the complexity of the material, the greater the students' experiences with DR-TA, the fewer the number of stopping points. *In the final analysis, the number of stopping points depends upon the teacher's assessment of the needs of the students.*

A few reading professionals have suggested analyzing the stories by story grammar and setting stopping points according to the results of the analysis. For example, a stopping point would be placed at the end of a descriptive portion of the material that deals with the story setting, another would be placed at the end of the climax, and so on. We believe strongly that such a practice is artificial at best, and one that does not capitalize on the ability of the teacher to assess the progress of the students. We have found teachers' judgement in determining stopping points, as well as deciding when stops should be skipped or added, to be competent, highly appropriate, and in keeping with the naturalness of the process embedded in DR-TAs.

Preplanning to ensure adequacy for the physical setting is also an important part of teacher preparation for a DR-TA. A major point to keep in mind concerns the facilitation of the group process. Students must be able to carry out face-to-face interactions with other group members. Does the seating arrangement provide for such communication? The teacher needs to sit with the group in a place that allows the teacher to see the students and facilitate and moderate the discussion. This role does not work as well if the teacher sits in the usual traditional place at the head of the group or if students sit in rows. The teacher may wish to sit at the side of the table or in a chair that is similar to the positions of other chairs in the group.

Maintain Teacher Consistency

The teacher's role of moderator/facilitator in the DR-TA means that the teacher *invites* students to participate in the discussion. The invitation to participate is offered to the whole group so that no one student feels singled out or pressured to talk. The question "Does anyone have a prediction regarding what will happen next?" is sometimes used to lead off the discussion. Students who are used to a traditional lesson that focuses on one correct response may be initially slow to participate, until they feel they understand their roles. Giving students an opportunity to feel comfortable in their roles may represent a critical point in the lesson. If the teacher breaks the consistency of the invitational pattern and calls on a student to talk, then students get confused. The signal they pick up says that they're really not invited; if they don't talk, they'll be called on. The rule of thumb: be patient and be silent.

Note how the teacher kept coming back to the invitation to participate in the following segment from a lesson:

T: WHAT DO YOU THINK THIS STORY'S GOING TO BE
            ABOUT?
S: umm
Brad: somebody's life
S: somebody...
T: OK.

50

T:	WHAT...CAN YOU BUILD ON THAT? CAN YOU TELL ME SOME MORE ABOUT THAT?
S:	it's her life
Tom:	a diary... it'll be a diary about life
S:	yeah
S:	could be a diary
T:	WHAT ELSE DO YOU THINK?
Tom:	Well it was about a lady..
T:	A LADY? WHAT DID IT DO?
Tom:	It was a life. It was about her life
T:	OK DO YOU WANT TO MAKE ANY PREDICTIONS ABOUT THAT LADY? CAN YOU TELL ME ANYTHING ABOUT...
S:	She's going to be older.
Tom:	She's old.
T:	WHY DO YOU SAY THAT?
S:	Well it's a story about her life.
Ss(2):	It says, All The Years...
S:	Yeah
S:	So that means that...
S:	So that means she's going to be like older?
T:	OK WHAT ELSE WOULD YOU LIKE TO GUESS THAT THIS MIGHT ABOUT?

The teacher in this lesson shows restraint. She is patient and accepting. The students' responses appear to be much like responses in a traditional lesson in that each response is short, students repeat what other students have said, or they pick up on something another student has said. Their responses show very little thinking that goes beyond the literal level. The teacher's use of the word ''guess'' is deliberate in her last question as she attempts to help them establish predictions. *It may take time for the students to become comfortable with the questioning patterns.* Teachers, then, may need to provide additional wait time and encouragement for responses. You may wish to keep notes on DR-TAs to view your own progress over time.

Some students in the group may not choose to initially respond to the teacher's questions, even when the questions have been phrased as invitations. If the students are given clues too limited for them to work with, they may need additional information in order to generate predictions. If the students aren't comfortable in their roles, be patient and be quiet. The students will work it out.

A frequent pitfall occurs when students don't readily make predictions and the teacher chooses to summarize what they've just read, based on the premise that if the students hear the summary, they will better understand what they read. The major problem with this choice is that *students are directed back into the material instead of forward into the material*. The process that students follow in a DR-TA is diagrammed below:

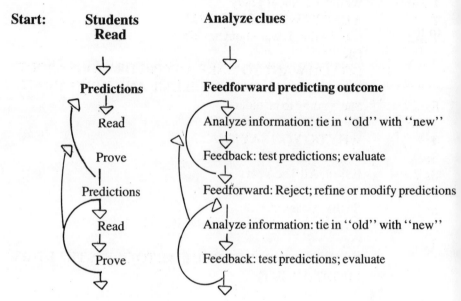

The act of making predictions will automatically carry students forward into the material because they have committed themselves to predictions with their peers. This commitment, combined with their own innate curiosity, causes a need to know. The teacher who holds up the process by summarizing actually can impede the students who may wonder if the teacher is attempting to cue them in some way.

Teachers must also take care not to reward predictions that they know will prove to be accurate in the material that has not yet been read. Students are skillful at picking up cues from the teacher; if they determine that the teacher is rewarding some predictions and not others, then the amount and quality of participation drops. In addition, students start paying attention to the teacher instead of the text. This shift in cognitive attention leads away from comprehension. All predictions should be encouraged and accepted by the teacher. After a story has been read, discussion of the predictions will help students look more critically at clues. Students need opportunities to piece together facts and information that ultimately lead to refined predictions.

When the teacher breaks off further prediction-setting after hearing an accurate prediction and and then directs the students to read, the teacher has reverted to the "question, response, feedback" pattern associated with the traditional DRA. This action not only breaks teaching consistency with the DR-TA, it sends a signal to the students that there is "one right answer" and that they must try to guess it. In the DR-TA, students need to examine all possibilities in their predictions, an essential component of problem-solving. The teacher should wait until the students show by their silence that they have no more predictions, signalling that they are ready to go on to the next step.

Teachers should carefully listen to students' predictions and the support they provide for those predictions. Student talk provides important information about how well students are comprehending the material. Some teachers wonder about how they will know if students really understand the material and, instead of carefully listening to the students, the teachers revert back to the comprehension assessment questions typical of the traditional DRA. This practice throws off students who weren't prepared to shift back to responding to "one correct response," it breaks the open communication network, and it sends a signal to students that they are no longer in a situation that has no fear of failure. Listening to students prove, reject, and refine predictions in discussion provides the teacher with an excellent view of students' comprehension. In the science transcript excerpt in Chapter II when students were discussing infrared, their initial predictions were off target. However, they discovered infrared wasn't a hot color; in fact, it wasn't even a color. You can tell from the discussion that comprehension has occurred.

Occasionally teachers think that the lesson is falling apart because they don't think the students are doing what they expect them to do. The teachers then revert back to asking traditional assessment questions and hope that by doing so, the students will have enough information to make predictions. These kinds of questions direct students *backward* into the story instead of *forward*.

Some students do not volunteer to participate during their first experiences with DR-TA. This troubles some teachers who think that everyone in the group *must* respond at some point in the lesson. We have found that when students have a need to talk they will do so. They do not have to respond verbally to be actively involved in the process of comprehension attainment. Most teachers find that as they observe students during the discussions and while they're reading, it is rare for students not to be involved. As students gain additional experiences with DR-TA, they tend to feel free to participate in discussions. When students feel the need to contribute, they will do so, *if the teacher maintains indirect influence and does not revert back to authoritarianism.* If the teacher forces students, they become suspicious and distrustful.

Asking Questions

Some teachers think that the only way to get students to respond to higher-level questions (application, synthesis, evaluation) is to begin with factual questions and work upward. That practice represents only *one* way; there are numerous alternatives. Students *can* respond to higher-level questions without first responding to factual questions. In order to adequately respond to a prediction question focused on text outcome, the students must process facts and other information in the content. We have found that the only time a factual question needs to be asked is if the student has misread information in the text or doesn't understand the concept being presented in the text.

One of the problems some teachers have encountered in early experiences using DR-TAs involves forgetting to ask students to support their responses. The two major questions in DR-TAs are "What do you think will happen?" and "Why do you think so?" or "What information in the material supports your prediction?" The first questions calls for students to generate predictions; the last two questions call for students to support their predictions. The power of the procedure lies in those two major questions. Teachers who challenge students to support the points or predictions they are raising are directing students to use the text for support along with their own experiential background. In time, most students tend habitually to support their predictions from information in the material.

Another problem with unsupported predictions is the signal they send to the group. If a prediction question is asked and a student's response is not supported, then other students think that any prediction, no matter how "off the wall" it seems, is appropriate. Asking students to support their responses with information gleaned from the material keeps them task-oriented and reading critically.

After students have read to a stop, teachers frequently ask students to identify any predictions that proved to be accurate and to share how they know. Stauffer (1969;1980) originally recommended that students should read the sentence that contains the proof. Most teachers find that students naturally tend to read only that portion of the sentence that contains the proof or recall that portion. Either is acceptable and preserves the naturalness of the discussion. Teachers who force students to read whole sentences or paragraphs find that the oral reading is choppy and stilted and, as a result, students make fewer predictions.

Some teachers ask questions that will help activate students' background knowledge. For example, a teacher using a story about dogs asked the students "How many of you have dogs at home?" Students began talking about their dogs, then other pets, and the teacher then had to stop them and direct the discussion back to the story being read. This type of question *leads away* from the material being read and the problem that they're solving.

54

Students' background knowledge is activated naturally in the DR-TA; they base their responses on information in the material being read and their knowledge of the world.

Another type of question that can cause potential problems is one that *leads students in a specific direction.* For example, a teacher having students read a story about a boy and a dragon, asked the students, "What do you think will happen to the dragon?" Students were directed toward only one part of the story. Those students who were exploring information about the boy thought they were "wrong" for investigating facts about the boy. In addition, *leading questions cause students to shift congitive attention to the teacher and the questions s/he may ask.*

Clarifying and elaborating types of questions, on the other hand, often enhance discussion, particularly if the student has responded with only two or three words. Asking for clarification and elaboration of a response allows students to articulate clearly what they are thinking about. Moreover, other students benefit from hearing the elaboration. There are several ways to get students to elaborate. Saying, "Talk a little more about that," is one of the simplest ways. It's important to phrase the sentence or question so that the student doesn't think that the response must be directed only to the teacher. For example, note the difference between "Talk a little more to me about that" and "talk a little more about that." One says *talk only to me;* the other says *share more information with us.*

Finally, *the art of asking questions in DR-TAs lies in listening closely to the students' responses and then asking questions that are based on those responses.* Note how the teacher follows up on students' responses in the following excerpts from transcripts of a lesson in science about light, color, and the spectrum.

T:	WHAT DO YOU EXPECT YOU WILL FIND?
	(Prediction question—open to anyone in the group to respond)
S1:	Heat
T:	WHY DO YOU SAY HEAT?
	(Asking student to support response)
S1:	Well, some of the colors are cooler.

Another type of question that can cause potential problems is one that *leads students in a specific direction.* For example, a teacher having students read a story about a boy and a dragon, asked the students, "What do you think will happen to the dragon?" Students were directed toward only one part of the story. Those students who were exploring information about the boy thought they were "wrong" for investigating facts about the boy. In addition, *leading questions cause students to shift congitive attention to the teacher and the questions s/he may ask.*

Clarifying and elaborating types of questions, on the other hand, often enhance discussion, particularly if the student has responded with only two or three words. Asking for clarification and elaboration of a response allows students to articulate clearly what they are thinking about. Moreover, other students benefit from hearing the elaboration. There are several ways to get students to elaborate. Saying, "Talk a little more about that," is one of the simplest ways. It's important to phrase the sentence or question so that the student doesn't think that the response must be directed only to the teacher. For example, note the difference between "Talk a little more to me about that" and "talk a little more about that." One says *talk only to me*; the other says *share more information with us.*

Finally, *the art of asking questions in DR-TAs lies in listening closely to the students' responses and then asking questions that are based on those responses.* Note how the teacher follows up on students' responses in the following excerpts from transcripts of a lesson in science about light, color, and the spectrum.

T:	WHAT DO YOU EXPECT YOU WILL FIND?
	(Prediction question—open to anyone in the group to respond)
S1:	Heat
T:	WHY DO YOU SAY HEAT?
	(Asking student to support response)
S1:	Well, some of the colors are cooler.
T:	DO YOU KNOW WHICH ONES ARE COOLER?
	(Asking for background knowledge of the student)
S1:	I think the darker ones.
T:	WHY DO YOU THINK THAT?
	(Asking student to support response)
S1:	They look cooler.
T:	OKAY. WHAT ELSE? DO YOU AGREE OR DISAGREE?
	(Asking for agreement, disagreement, and new predictions)
S2:	Well, I agree with her on infrared and ultraviolet. They are probably the hottest colors you can get in the spectrum.
T:	All RIGHT. ANYBODY ELSE?
	(Asking for agreement or disagreement.)
S3:	I think he's wrong.
T:	WHY?
	(Asking student to support response)

S3:	Because whenever you melt steel, steel always turns red before it turns white. When it turns white, it melts completely.
S4:	You can't see infrared.
T:	AND HOW WOULD THAT MAKE A DIFFERENCE IN WHAT HE JUST SAID?
	(Analysis question)
S4:	Well, he just said that it turned red before it turned white. And really you can't see white, it's just a shade. Infrared you can't see—which would be just like sunlight, you can't see sunlight, so I think it would be hotter.

In discussions in many classes, the teacher would have simply judged the students' responses as correct or incorrect and *then told them the correct answers or called on other students until correct responses had been given.* Had the teacher, in the lesson above, not followed up on the students' responses, she would have had absolutely no notion of what they were thinking about or basing their responses on and absolutely no notion of their understanding of the concepts being presented in the text. Look at the length of the students' responses. They go well beyond the ''standard'' two to three word responses made in many traditional DRAs. Moreover, the students are not only using the language of the discipline, they're learning how to agree intellectually and disagree with one another. Meanwhile, the teacher has achieved complete consistency in maintaining the open communication network and encouraging students to interact.

Regulating the Amount of Information

Varying the amount of information students read at one time is important in keeping lessons fresh. If students always make predictions based on the title, they get bored. It is also possible to place so many stops in the material that the students get impatient and want to go ahead. When students ask, ''Can't we read on?'' and they're not referring to the fact that they're excited and want to find out if their predictions are accurate, then it may be a sure signal that they're bored.

Some students read at a slower pace than others. Teachers frequently ask, ''Should we wait for all students to finish before starting the discussion?'' There are two points to be considered in answering this question. The first point is to make certain that the material is at the instructional level of the lowest reader in the group. If this need is met, then we suggest that teachers wait to start the discussion until almost all students have completed the reading. We have found that students who have not finished will do so before they join the discussion. We suggest telling students who read more rapidly, to sit quietly and think about what they've read while they're waiting for others to finish. This suggestion places value on thinking. Students who finish more rapidly than others also frequently seem to enjoy watching the expressions on others' faces as they read.

Well-placed stops that have been predetermined along with optional stops tend to provide the teacher with enough choices to meet the needs of the students. Alternative stopping points should always be determined. Sometimes students have difficulty making predictions because they don't have enough information. Sometimes students' interests are so high that a number of stopping points can be skipped. By predetermining alternate stopping points, the teacher is free to use them when students need more information in order to form predictions or fee to stop them when students' interests are high. As stated earlier in Chapter I, stops should be planned to meet the students' needs as they read. The lesson should flow smoothly; discussion should be an integral part of the lesson. As students grow in experience with the procedure, they will need fewer stops for discussion depending on the complexity of the material.

Maintaining Integrity of the DR-TA

Maintaining integrity of the procedure is important to the success of the lesson. There are a number of modifications of the DR-TA that change it so radically that it can no longer be called a DR-TA.

One of these changes we have observed involves "round robin predicting." The teacher calls on each student around the circle to make a prediction. Then they read. The reason for the changes is apparently to involve all students in the prediction process. However, note that the open-communication network associated with DR-TA is not evident nor is the problem-solving process. Students are talking to and thinking about the teacher, not the text. Students are simply doing what is being asked of them: making predictions. There is no individual intellectual commitment to predicting and then proving the prediction. The students are following out the teacher's orders. Round robin predicting changes the procedure; therefore, it should not be referred to as a DR-TA.

The move towards increasing student writing has been the basis of another practice that hinders the DR-TA: namely, writing predictions. Having students stop to write predictions, then read them to the group introduces a destructive dimension to the DR-TA. The spontaneity of discussion is seriously jeopardized; students begin to concentrate on spelling, syntax, and handwriting; slower students feel penalyzed; all of which can break the train of thought they had established as they read and analyzed. For all these reasons, one must also seriously question whether the practice of writing during a DR-TA is pedagogically sound. Writing activities are often effective in Step V.

Occasionally teachers say that they write the students' predictions on the chalkboard. Again, we must question why the discussion must be interrupted for this practice. Students have no problems recalling predictions; in fact, they claim group ownership of some of them. This happens in the spirit of group cohesiveness and group pride in a job well done. Both students' writing and teachers' writing also make predictions seem like permanent products and not a part of the process of constructing meaning.

There is an old adage that applies to such modifications: If it works, don't fix it! The DR-TA is a procedure that works. Tinkering with the proceaure generally interferes with the problem-solving process.

Some points to keep in mind when teaching DR-TAs are as follows:

1. The open-communication structure must be evident throughout the lesson.

2. There should be at least as much, if not more, student talk than teacher talk.

3. Students should be encouraged to make as many predictions as possible that are relevant to the material.

4. Students must provide reasoning and support for their responses.

5. Discussion is an essential part of the procedure.

6. The teacher should be firmly in the role of moderator, intellectual agitator, and facilitator.

Implementing DR-TAs is not easy for many teachers. They find it difficult to step completely out of the more traditional teacher role associated with the DRA. When DR-TAs don't seem to go well, it might be helpful to audio- or videotape the next one in order to analyze it at a later time to pinpoint problems. It may also be helpful to use Chapter II as a guideline for analyzing your own lessons. Anoter possibility would be to ask a colleague knowledgeable about DR-TAs to come in and observe. However, even without prior experience on the part of the teacher, even without prior experience on the part of the students, students' responses during DR-TAs reflect more higher-level thinking than during the traditional DRA (Petre, 1970; Davidson, 1970, Rusnak, 1983; Wilkerson, 1984). The important thing is to keep trying.

CHAPTER IV

WHAT WE KNOW ABOUT THE USE OF DR-TA

The DR-TA has come into its own during the past decade, even though the procedure is over twenty years old. We will discuss in this chapter what we know about the use of the DR-TA. The procedure has been the subject of a number of research studies, and research has some important ramifications for group instruction with the DR-TA. The statements found in this chapter are all supported by research investigations, particularly those by Davidson, Padak, and Wilkerson. A summary of the research appears in the next chapter.

Four basic premises are associated with DR-TAs. They are as follows:

Premise One: Learning is a social process.

Premise Two: Students need maximum opportunities to interact with one another in the use of language associated with the task.

Premise Three: Meaning is constructed through the interaction of students, teacher, and text.

Premise Four: Comprehension attainment requires active involvement from learners.
(Davidson, 1986)

These premises serve as guidelines for instruction with the use of DR-TAs. Note how they are interwoven in the learners' role, the process associated with DR-TAs, the teacher's role in the process, and the overall learning product.

The Learners' Role in DR-TA

Students are actively involved in the learning process: hypothesizing and purpose-setting; sifting and analyzing information; examining facts, making judgements; all in the search for meaning and understanding. Cooperative student participation is a crucial aspect of the DR-TA lesson; the open communication structure fosters cooperative involvement and interaction among the students, and with the teacher, in the lesson. The teacher and the students, through their interactions, determine their roles in the lesson. We have found that both the teacher's and students' roles require asking questions and offering responses. As students and teacher interact cooperatively with one another, they work together in constructing meaning.

Students participating in DR-TAs care about learning and accept the responsibility for development of comprehension. Their role is not to receive information, but to create learning through analysis of information they both receive and make available. Students bear the responsibility of extracting information, assimilating, sharing, and comprehending. Their role is one which is empowered, motivated, and invested through individual purpose setting. Students' introspections following participation in DR-TAs reflect involvement in concept analysis and development during the lessons and continuing involvement in related problem solving after the lessons. This is in contrast to the involvement of students in the more traditional DRA, who report more attention during the lessons to procedural concerns, i.e., thinking about answers to questions the teacher might ask, as well as a greater tendency to fail to report involvement with concepts during the lesson.

Students not only tend to talk more and take longer turns during DR-TAs than they do during DRAs, but they also consistently use information provided by others to make sense of concepts. In addition, students provide links within and among information and concepts in the text. It's not unusual for ideas and possibilities offered early in a lesson to be referred to and evaluated at later points in the lesson. Students remember their own and others' thinking; thus, group members' thought becomes a valuable, communal resource for learning. The learner's role in DR-TAs is one of effectively using all available resources: the text, prior experience, and the thinking of others revealed through group discussion to develop concepts and create understanding.

The Learning Process

The learning process in DR-TAs is a cooperative, generative process of concept development. The key elements in the process are purpose setting and critical analysis of text through discussion. Use of DR-TAs provides a means for actively involving students in the search for meaning and creates an environment of individual investment in learning. The teacher and students *share* responsibility for the lesson, with the students assuming that responsibility *at the onset of the lesson*. The lesson involves a cycled process of students hypothesizing, analyzing hypotheses, and then evaluating them in terms of the text and the students' prior knowledge. Group discussion occurs

61

in an open communication group structure which tends to foster cooperative involvement among the participants. The process of hypothesizing in the group causes students to make commitments to learning. They have a *need* to find out if their hypotheses are accurate.

The following figure shows the difference in the learning process between the DR-TA and the more traditional DRA:

Figure 6
Student Involvement in the Learning Process
(Davidson, Padak, & Wilkerson, 1986b.)

DRA	DR-TA
Passive	Active
Isolated	Cooperative
Teacher focus	Content focus
Sequential accumulation of text facts	Integrative, evaluative process of inquiry

Note the difference in the focus of the two instructional strategies. Students participating in the more traditional DRA tend to focus on the teacher; students participating in a DR-TA tend to focus more on the content of the lesson. The pattern of teacher questions in a DR-TA tends to prompt and encourage students to integrate concepts for themselves. Their talk tends to show that they are linking concepts back to other concepts previously discussed, thus integrating or identifying relationships between and among the text concepts.

The Teacher's Role

The teacher serves as the moderator and facilitator of the group. The teacher encourages students to formulate their own purposes and group purposes through hypothesizing. The process actually begins when the teacher selects the material that is to be read by the students. The teacher reads the text, interprets concepts in the text material, and plans how to facilitate students' interpretations of those concepts. The teacher's role is that of *facilitator,* rather than that of the "giver of information." The teacher plans stopping points in the reading, and acts as the "intellectual agitator," asking students to formulate predictions, elaborate, explain, clarify, and prove. The teacher encourages students to take intellectual risks: there is no fear of failure since the teacher regulates the amount of information read at one time and the outcome is unknown until they read the material. The cycle of purpose setting, reading according to purposes set, and redefining purposes occurs within an open communication structure facilitated by the teacher. The teacher facilitates concept development through physical arrangement of the group, adjustment of group size, and by listening to students, taking cues from their discussion.

The teacher talk in DR-TAs tends to show less tendency to introduce "new" information since the students are doing this themselves. The quantity of teacher talk during a DR-TA shows that teacher turns are about as long as the students. However, in the more traditional DRA the teacher provides newer or previously undiscussed concepts for the students, provides additional explicit content, and talks from 2 to 9 times longer than the students. The critical element here concerns the fact that *most of the teacher's talk during DR-TAs is based on the students' responses and most of the teacher's talk during the more traditional DRA concerns giving information or content to students.*

Products of Learning

We have found consistent evidence that differences in instruction make a difference in student learning. In DR-TAs members of the instructional group work toward the instructional goal through a process of analytical verbal interaction about the text being read. Students participating in DR-TAs are involved in generating critical responses to text and are highly task-oriented toward goal attainment. Through this dynamic process, students create and develop a product of understanding and comprehension. DR-TAs have been shown to facilitate comprehension of major generalizations intended by the text and the tying of textual information to prior knowledge to a greater extent than traditional DRAs. As a result of participating in DR-TAs, students tend to comprehend textual concepts and apply generalizations in the text to concepts that go beyond the scope of the text. Our studies (Davidson, Padak, & Wilkerson) show that one day following the lessons, students are still engaged in problem solving about the text concepts. This is in contrast to the more traditional DRA, in which the passive nature of the learning process, coupled with the focus on the teacher, does not appear to encourage students to go beyond the scope of the text or process information in a manner which provides for retention and analysis of text concepts.

We have found that students' comprehension is facilitated to a greater extent through involvement in DR-TAs than through DRAs whether the teacher of the lesson is a reading teacher or a teacher specializing in the content being addressed. This was true even when the DRA was the content specialist's normal lesson structure. Such results emphasize the importance of the instructional strategy or structure in facilitating students' comprehension of text. In DR-TAs the "cognitive work" is the responsibility of students. The product is critical response to text.

All of these elements associated with DR-TAs interrelate in creating an effective instructional procedure that facilitates students' reading and critical thinking. Use of DR-TAs results in facilitation of the students' processes of comprehension attainment of text material. Students are free to think, to test, and to learn. They are responsible for analyzing, evaluating, and providing proof of their judgments as they are involved in the process of critically comprehending text "until the constructs or concepts presented are clearly grasped, critically evaluated, accepted and applied, or rejected" (Stauffer, 1969, p 16).

CHAPTER V

A SUMMARY OF RESEARCH

Introduction

Ernest Horn's (1937) discussion of reading, written almost fifty years ago, presents a description of the reading task that is relevant for teachers and researchers concerned with comprehension today. Horn, writing about methods of instruction in social studies, stated:

"The author ... does not really convey ideas to the reader, he merely stimulates him to construct them out of his own experience. If the concept is already in the reader's mind, the talk is relatively easy, but if, as is usually the case in school, it is new to the reader, its construction more nearly approaches problem-solving than simple association. Moreover, any error, bias, or inadequacy in the author's statement is almost certain to be reflected in the ideas formed by the student." (Horn, 1937, p. 154)

Influenced by such contemporaries as Piaget and Bruner, Stauffer (1970) provided an additional contribution to the description of the reading task: "...critical reading like critical thinking requires cognitive interaction between facts and values, hypotheses and proofs, and results in internalization of knowledge and self-regulation" (p. 13). According to Stauffer (1975) the structure of the reading-thinking process is governed by and dependent upon the interplay of the reader's anticipation and the confirmation or denial that he or she obtains. Two key Piagetian concepts are cited by Stauffer: action and interaction. He then added a third concept, transaction. He emphasizes the social nature of learning which requires children to act and communicate or interact with each other; transactions occur through communication, as well.

The process of making interpretations and generating inferences is enhanced in an ego-supporting climate of an instructional group with open lines of communication (Taba, 1962; Spache, 1968) where the teacher acts as a facilitator and moderates the group. Current investigations of the reading process and comprehension focus on the reader interacting with text, often neglecting the role of the contextual setting in the process being investigated. The necessity for combining comprehension research with exploration of reading instruction in a contextual setting (Duffy, 1980) is based on the premise that learning is a social process and that reading instruction involves social interaction (Bloome, 1985; Cazden, 1981).

The summary of research concerns the DR-TA in contextual settings. Some of the studies focus on the interactions of the teacher and the students, comparing the DR-TA and the traditional DRA. More recent studies focus on the roles of both students and teachers in the interactions and emphasize the interactions among students as well as with the teacher.

DR-TA Research

One of the earliest investigations related to DR-TA was conducted by Henderson (1963) who was concerned with the purpose-setting behaviors of two groups of 24 fifth graders. Based on evidence from the investigation, Henderson concluded that pupil purpose-setting does make a difference in achievement.

Petre (1970) compared the quantity, quality, and variety of responses of 120 fourth graders in 24 groups, five students per group, who participated in DRAs and DR-TAs. Responses were classified according to the Ohio Scales (Wolf, King & Huck, 1967). Results showed students' responses during the DR-TA were superior whether the children were at, above, or below grade level in reading achievement.

Davidson (1970) replicated Petre's study with 90 fourth graders and extended it to include the kinds of questions asked by teachers during the two procedures. Results showed teachers using the DR-TA asked chiefly interpreting, inferring (prediction) types of questions; teachers using the DRAs tended to ask chiefly factual types of questions. Davidson's conclusions supported those of Petre's; that students' responses during the DR-TAs were at levels that represented critical thinking. Moreover, interpreting, inferring (prediction) types of questions tended to stimulate responses involving hypothesizing or predicting and theorizing; evaluative types of questions tended to stimulate responses that involved making decisions or judgements based on some logical criteria. These results were similar to the findings of Wolf, Huck, and King (1967) in their classic study of children's thinking.

Grobler (1970) examined the methodology in reading instruction as a controlled variable in the constructive or destructive channeling of aggression. Subjects were fourth graders receiving instruction in either DR-TAs or DRAs. Four observers rated the students' behavior on a constructive-neutral-destructive rating scale. Independent variables were method, I.Q., reading level, and sex. Findings showed that students instructed in DR-TAs displayed significantly more constructive behavior than students in DRAs. Grobler also found that DR-TAs were more effective in producing relatively more constructive behavior in low I.Q. students.

Biskin, Hoskisson, and Modlin (1976), working with first- and third-grade Title I students, compared students' recall after being taught stories by means of a DR-TA and after listening to the stories without discussion. Results showed the students remembered story elements better after a DR-TA.

Stauffer (1976) reported results of a sixth-year longitudinal study which concerned comprehension as achieved by means of global language-experience procedures. The study began with Stauffer's participation in the USOE beginning reading studies. Results were reported each year for the first three years (Stauffer & Hammond, 1965, 1966, 1969) and a fiscal report was made at the end of the children's sixth year in school (Stauffer, Hammond, Oehlkers, & Houseman, 1976). DR-TAs were an important part of the instructional procedures each year of the study. Stauffer concluded that first-grade children in the experimental group achieved significantly better in paragraph meaning and word reading than did children in the control group as measured by the Stanford Achievement Test, and in Word Study Skills they did as well as children in the control group.

Extended into the second grade, children in the experimental group achieved significantly better on word meaning, paragraph meaning, spelling, and word skills as measured by the Stanford. Extended into third grade, no significant differences in word knowledge and reading were found between the two groups. Stauffer pointed out that the Stanford subtests required only a limited facility in reading; questions were usually literal rather than inferential. The overall test format was similar to the format in basal readers and workbooks which may have minimized differences between the groups.

The final report, at the end of the sixth year, showed no significant differences between the two groups in word knowledge and reading. Stauffer suggested that the tests were inadequate in assessing the students' performance in these areas. Teachers' judgements about the students' reading performance, however, were markedly different from test results. Teachers pointed clearly to students' critical reading abilities. Stauffer concluded that attributes of a critical reader were almost totally unmeasured except for teacher judgement. He emphasized the need for appropriate tests and the need for research funds for longitudinal studies.

Homer (1977) examined the influence on reading behavior of two purpose-setting procedures for administering an informal reading inventory to 38 fourth grade pupils: individually formulated pupil purposes for reading, elicited by the questioning format used in purpose-setting in a DR-TA and a priori purposes for reading stated in the examiner's manual. Two formats of the Standard Reading Inventory (McCracken, 1966) were used to determine reading achievement levels. Findings showed that when reading was directed by individually formulated pupil purposes, reading achievement levels were significantly higher and spanned a higher and wider range of grade levels on the informal reading inventory. Conclusions supported Henderson's (1963) finding regarding individual purpose-setting and general reading achievement, and Davidson's (1970) findings concerning the relationship between teachers' questions and students' responses.

Hammond (1979) studied the effects of 60 fifth-grade students' predictions on prequestions in the recall of relevant and incidental information found in expository material. Students were randomly assigned to two groups. One group read questions and were told they would be tested on the questions after the reading; the second group read questions and predicted answers to the questions by means of the questioning format used in purpose-setting in a DR-TA. Groups read passages, answered questions, and then answered an additional set of questions. Results showed that predictions used with prequestions significantly increased the recall of relevant information and incidental information.

Padak (1982) investigated the quantity, quality, and variety of inferences generated in DR-TAs and Group Mapping Activities (GMAs). DR-TAs were used to present the reading materials to students; GMAs were used as a 5th Step Activity and served as catalysts for discussion after the DR-TA. Findings showed that DR-TAs tended to promote inferences about motivation and causation. GMAs promoted evaluative inferences. Padak concluded that DR-TAs and GMAs are powerful when used together.

Rusnak (1983) replicated Davidson's 1970 study and examined the relationship between teachers' questions and students' responses during a DRA and a DR-TA. Subjects were 144 third-grade students. Findings supported those of Davidson's. A relationship existed between teachers' questions and students' responses; teachers tended to ask more interpreting (prediction) questions during the DR-TA; during the DRA more factual questions were asked by teachers; and, even without prior experience with the procedure, students' responses were superior regardless whether they were reading at, above, or below grade level. Teachers also asked more higher-level questions during the DR-TA, even without prior experience. Rusnak concluded that the use of the DR-TA tends to facilitate higher level question asking from teachers.

Draheim (1984) investigated the facilitation of comprehension and written recall of expository text through DR-TA and conceptual mapping with two groups of college freshmen. She set up three training cycles: each cycle included DR-TAs, mapping, discussion, and the writing of an essay based on an expository text. Draheim concluded that average and poor students who participated in DR-TAs, made conceptual maps, and then wrote essays could recall more main ideas from reading than students in the control group. She suggested that DR-TAs and mapping appear to help students recall ideas needed during the writing of thesis-support and summary-analysis writing tasks.

Pinter (1985) examined the effect of text simplification and instructional procedure on the inference generation on fifth grade disabled readers. The

DR-TA instructional procedure was compared with the traditional DRA. The Group Mapping Activity (GMA) served as a catalyst for discussion following both procedures. The DR-TA stimulated students to generate significantly more inferences than students in the DRA. The GMA facilitated more inference generation from students when preceded by the DR-TA than the DRA. The DR-TA discussion resulted in more logical inferences and fewer informational inferences than the DRA discussion. Pinter concluded that the quantity, type, and validity of inferences are affected by the nature of the task involved within an instructional setting. Subjects who participated in the DR-TA made fewer invalid inferences than those in the DRA. No differences in quantity, type, and validity resulted from text simplification. The DR-TA was described by Pinter as an effective catalyst for inference generation for followup activities.

Padak and Padak (1987) examined high-school students' written reactions to DR-TAs conducted during a three-month period. The teachers' written reflections about instruction were also examined. They found that the teacher perceives qualitative differences in lessons. Over time students elaborated more freely, predicted more fully, and used prior knowledge more effectively to construct meaning through discussions. Examination of students' written reactions to stories revealed that students became more evaluative and showed more evidence of critical judgement as their experiences with DR-TAs broadened.

Lia (1988) examined second-grade students' inferences during three types of story reading sessions. The three types of lessons were the Directed Listening-Thinking Activity (DL-TA) in which the students participated in a DR-TA with the story read aloud to them; a Directed Listening Activity (DLA) in which the students participated in a DRA with the story read aloud to them; and, a Whole Text Method (WTM) in which the story was simply read aloud to them without discussion. Findings showed that students participating in the DL-TA generated more inferences than students in the other groups. Lia concluded that all three types of lessons stimulated inferences from students and that the read aloud sessions had value for instructional purposes in comprehension. Lia also concluded that use of the DL-TA was particularly successful.

The Davidson, Padak, & Wilkerson Studies

Davidson, Padak, & Wilkerson, working singly and cooperatively, have conducted a line of investigations during the past seven years concerning the process of comprehension attainment with eighth-grade students in science, social studies, and literature lessons. The following summary concerns their major investigations.

Sex differences in the verbal leadership behavior of eighth-grade students, four males and four females, during a DR-TA was investigated by Wilkerson (Greenslade, 1982). Subjects were videotaped as they participated in a DR-TA in literature. Statistically significant differences were found in the quantity of verbalizations of males and females. Males talked more than females during the first half of the activity; however, females achieved equal status in the quantity of verbalizations during the last half of the activity. Females took a supportive role during the first half of the activity while males took leadership roles. During the last half of the activity, females began to take the initiative in leadership and did so to the extent that the overall difference was not significant. Females showed more task orientation. Greenslade (Wilkerson), although noting that generalizations from the study must be made with caution due to the small size of the sample, suggested that the DR-TA may be facilitative of leadership development in both females and males.

Wilkerson (Greenslade, 1982) studied the relationship of quantity, quality, and variety of verbalizations and task-orientation in a group DR-TA. Subjects were four male and four female eighth grade students who were videotaped as they participated in the DR-TA. Wilkerson concluded that a relationship existed between critical level responses and task orientation. Critical level responses tended to be task-oriented; responses representing non-critical levels of thinking tended to be non-task-oriented. Wilkerson concluded further that the DR-TA process stimulated task-oriented behavior from the students as well as critical levels of response to text.

Wilkerson (1984) described and compared the process of comprehension attainment of social studies text material during two group reading activities, the Directed Reading-Thinking Activity (DR-TA) and the Directed Reading Activity (DRA). Inferences during the group activities and during individual post reading and introspective reports were examined. Two groups of eight eighth grade students read the same segment from a social studies text customarily used in their social studies instruction, but from a unit they had not previously used. Lessons were videotaped; interviews were audiotaped. Transcripts of the lessons, postreading interviews, and introspective reports were analyzed to determine the quantity and types of inferences generated by each group in each assessment context and to determine the quantity and types of information included in inferences. A qualitative taxonomy of inferences, developed from descriptive schemes proposed by Taba, Durkin, Fraenkel, and McNaughton (1971) was used for categorization of inferences and information included in inferences. Wilkerson concluded that the process of comprehension was different in the DR-TA and the DRA. The DR-TA was superior in encouraging interaction of students' prior knowledge with textual material and in facilitating students' generalizing beyond the textual

70

information.

Davidson (1985) investigated eighth-grade students' introspections of discussions in science and social studies lessons. Subjects were four groups of eight eighth-grade students; each group was evenly matched with girls and boys. Two of the groups received instructional lessons described as Teacher-Student Generated Lessons in which the text material in science and in social studies was presented by means of a DR-TA. The other two groups received instructional lessons described as Teacher Manual Generated Lessons in which the text material in science and social studies was presented in a closed-communication structure following the instructional suggestions in the manuals of the two texts. The lessons were videotaped and transcribed for purposes of analysis. Oral recalls of important generalizations were individually collected and audiotaped the day following the lessons. The students then viewed the appropriate videotapes. At stopping points in the discussion, the videotape playback was halted and individual interviews were conducted with each of the students. They were asked to tell what they were thinking about during the discussion. These oral introspections were audiotaped and transcriptions were made for purposes of analysis.

Davidson concluded that the major difference in students' introspections after TMGLs and TSGLs seems to lie in students' purposes for reading, determined by the two instructional procedures. Students in TMGLs read what they had been asked to read. They "fed back" bits of text to the teacher. Results showed that these students were engaged in "mock participation" (Bloome, 1983), or in other words, they looked like they were involved in the task. However, a number of their introspections dealt with comments classified as "schooling" in that they dealt with behavior (i.e. "You have to pay attention ... you don't want to get in trouble."). Many comments of students in these groups indicated that they were "thinking of answers to questions that the teacher might ask."

Students who participated in DR-TAs set their own purposes for reading, read to find out if their predictions were accurate or needed to be reformulated or rejected. The students were actively involved in the learning process. Davidson reported, "Teacher-Student Generated Lessons, such as those based on the Directed Reading-Thinking Activity, stimulate greater involvement from students who work together in discussions in order to attain understanding of concepts" (p. 243).

Padak (1985) examined teachers' verbal patterns and decision-making, with specific attention given to the influence of the instructional setting. She found that instructional setting did influence teachers' decision-making. During the Teacher-Manual Generated Lessons (TMGL) in which a DRA was used, teachers took major responsibility for the lessons. During the Teacher-Student Generated Lessons (TSGL) in which a DR-TA was used,

71

the responsibility for the lessons was shared by the teacher and the students. The teacher directed the discussions during the TMGLs; the teacher and the students, working together, directed the discussions in the TSGLs.

Davidson, Padak, & Wilkerson (1985) explored the relationships between the instructional contexts of reading and discussion in eighth-grade literature classes compared with science and social studies classes. The study focused on the unfolding of instructional contexts during one pair of English lessons taught by a reading teacher; two pairs of science lessons, one taught by a reading teacher and one taught by a science teacher; and, one pair of social studies lessons taught by a reading teacher. The same text was used for each pair of lessons. However, the instructional framework differed within each pair of lessons: one lesson was based on the teacher's interpretations of the content and suggestions for instruction identified in the teacher's manual, labelled a Teacher-Manual Generated Lesson (TMGL) and the other lesson was based on a problem-solving procedure, the DR-TA, labelled a Teacher-Student Generated Lesson (TSGL). The lessons were videotaped; students' retrospective introspections and recall of what they were thinking were collected 24 hours later by showing and discussing the appropriate videotape. Teacher introspections and recalls were collected in a similar manner. Transcripts were made of the lessons and the recall sessions. Students' maps drawn following the discussions in the literature lessons were collected for purposes of analysis. Data analysis included: (1) analyzing transcripts for patterns of inferences generated within each lesson; (2) microethnographic analyses (Green & Wallat, 1981) of the transcriptions and videotapes that led to the development of structural maps of the socio-communicative behaviors for each of the lessons; (3) quantitative analysis of the amount of talk, number and types of questions, interactional units, and concept-linking statements; (4) analysis of teacher decision-making within each lesson; (5) a comparative analysis of what students were thinking about, compared with elements identified in the lesson that was evolving; and, (6) classification of maps. Factors are identified that contribute to the reading curriculum in each of the lessons. Findings from all lessons are summarized in Figure 1. The terms Teacher-Manual Generated Lessons (TMGL) and Teacher-Student Generated Lessons (TSGL) are used because the emphasis in all the studies was to examine differences in instructional frameworks. However, the DRA was the lesson type used in the Teacher-Manual Generated Lessons and the DR-TA was the lesson typed used in the Teacher-Student Generated Lessons. The focus in the TMGLs in which the DRA was used seemed to be primarily on the teacher. In contrast, during TSGLs in which the DR-TA was used, the focus seemed to be primarily on the learners interacting with the text. In the final analysis, only the DR-TA in the Teacher-Student Generated

Lessons stimulated students to become actively involved in the process of comprehension attainment of text.

Figure 7
Teacher-Manual Generated Lessons (TMGLs)
and Teacher-Student Generated Lessons (TSGLs):
Summary of Findings (Padak & Davidson, 1988)

Patterns of Interaction During The Lessons	TMGLs	TSGLs
Emphasis of discussion *d, e*	After reading portions of text	Before reading portions of text
Control of discussion *g, h, i*	Teacher directed discussion	Teacher and student directed discussion
Communication patterns *e*	Students tended to talk only to teacher	Students tended to talk to teacher and each other
Verbal contributions *e, i*	Dominated by teacher (T: 68-84%)	Shared among all participants (T: 37-47%)
Content of Interactions During The Lessons		
Typical question/ response *e, f*	Factual question/ literal response	Predicting or evaluating question/critical response
Integration of content and concepts *c, g, h, i*	Primarily teacher's responsibility; most linking comments back to teacher's	Primarily student responsibility; most linking comments back to students' contributions contributions
Student inferences *j, k, l*	Closely tied to text information; little elaboration or evaluation of text material	Attempted to link text information with prior knowledge; elaborated upon and evaluated text information
Effect on Students		
Apparent learning *j, k, l*	In general, recalled facts but failed to demonstrate	In general, recalled facts; demonstrated comprehension

73

	comprehension of major text generalizations	of major text generalizations
Reported thoughts: *a, b*		
Text-related	27-30%	60-64%
Lesson-related	24-43%	13-15%
Can't remember	17-27%	0-4 %

a: Davidson, 1985; b: Davidson, 1986; c: Davidson, 1987; d: Davidson, Padak, & Wilkerson, 1986a; e: Davidson, Padak, & Wilkerson, 1986b; f: Davidson, Padak, & Wilkerson, 1987; g: Padak, 1985; h: Padak, 1986; i: Padak, 1987; j: Wilkerson, 1984; k: Wilkerson, 1986; l: Wilkerson, 1987

The hidden curriculum (Cook-Gumperz & Gumperz, 1982) refers to the assumptions students make about what is important to learn and how to learn. In interacting with one another and the teacher, students gather signals that may or may not be what the teacher intended to convey about learning. Figure 2 shows aspects of the hidden curriculum in Teacher-Manual Generated Lessons (TMGL) and Teacher-Student Generated Lessons (TSGL). The DR-TA was the instructional strategy used in the TSGL curricular framework. Results of the Davidson, Padak, & Wilkerson studies suggest that in TMGLs in which DRAs are used, students may gather signals that indicate to them that it is important to learn facts and answer questions asked by the teacher. On the other hand, students in TSGLs in which DR-TAs were used, may gather signals that indicate that quality thinking is important and that understanding the text is also important.

Figure 8
TMGLs and TSGLs:
Aspects of the Hidden Curriculum*
(Padak & Davidson, 1988)

	TMGLs	TSGLs
What's Important to Learn:	It's important to learn what's in the text	It's important to evaluate new information in light of what is already known
How Does One Learn?	One learns by listening to the teacher, answering the teacher's questions, and relying on the teacher to provide important information and generalizations	One learns by listening to and cooperating with others in the group and by working together to explore important information and generalizations

* Davidson, Padak, & Wilkerson, 1987

Conclusion

The summary of investigations about DR-TA shows evidence that supports the use of the procedure as a means of facilitating students' processes of comprehension attainment. There may be other studies concerning DR-TA that are not known to us at this time. All the studies cited in this summary show that the DR-TA facilitates students' critical thinking. Moreover, students are actively involved in the learning process when they are engaged in DR-TAs, they have a need to know, and they care about learning. The research summarized demonstrates that the group problem-solving process that is facilitated during DR-TAs has applications for comprehending text in science, social studies, and literature.

Abercrombie, M. L. J. (1985). *The Anatomy of Judgement*. New York: Viking Penguin, Inc.

Alvermann, Donna E., Dillon, Deborah R., and O'Brien, David G. (1987). *Using Discussion To Promote Reading Comprehension*. Newark, DE: International Reading Association.

Bales, Robert F. (1950). *Interaction Process Analysis*. Cambridge,Mass.: Addison-Wesley Press, Inc.

Bavelas, Alex (1950). Communication Patterns in Task-oriented Groups. *Journal of the Acoustical Society of America*, vol. 22, pp. 725-730.

Berry, Kathleen S. (1985). Talking to Learn Subject Matter/Learning Subject Matter Talk. *Language Arts*, vol. 64, pp. 34-42.

Betts, Emmett A. (1946). *Foundations of Reading Instruction*. New York: American Book Co.

Biskin, D. S., Hoskisson, K., & Modlin, M. (1976). Prediction, Reflection, and Comprehension. *Elementary School Journal*, vol. 77, pp. 131-139.

Bloome, David. (1985). Reading As a Social Process. *Language Arts*, vol. 62, pp. 134-142.

Bloome, David (1984). A Socio-communicative Perspective of Formal and Informal Classroom Reading Events. In J.A. Niles & L.A. Harris (Eds.), *Changing Perspectives on Research in Reading/Language Processing and Instruction*. Rochester, NY: National Reading Conference.

Bloome, David. (1983). Classroom Reading Instruction: A Socio-communicative Analysis of Time on Task. In J. A. Niles & L. A. Harris (Eds.), *Searches for Meaning in Reading/Language Processing & Instructon*. Thirty-second Yearbook of the National Reading Conference. Rochester, NY: National Reading Conference.

Bruner, Jerome. (1978). The Role of Dialogue in Language Acquisition. In A. Sinclair, R. J. Jarvelle, & W. J. M. Levelt (Eds.), *The Child's Concept of Language*. New York: Springer-Verlag.

Cazden, Courtney B. (1981). Social Context of Learning to Read. In J. T. Guthrie (Ed.), *Comprehension and Teaching: Research Views*. Newark, DE: International Reading Association.

Cook-Gumperz, Jennie, and Gumperz, John (1982). Communicative Competence in Educational Perspective. In L.C. Wilkinson (Ed.), *Communicating in the Classroom*. New York: Academic Press.

Courtney, Brother Leonard (1968). Critical-creative Reading in the Secondary Schools. *Development of lifetime Reading Habits*. Newark, DE: International Reading Association.

Davidson, Jane L. (1987). *A Comparison of Patterns of Teacher-Student Communicative Behaviors in Junior High Literature Lessons*. Paper presented at the American Educational Research Association Conference, Washington, DC, April.

Davidson, Jane L. (1986). The Teacher-student Generated Lesson: A Model for Reading Instruction. *Theory into Practice*, vol. 25, (Spring) pp. 84-90.

Davidson, Jane L. (1985). What You Think Is Going On, Isn't: Eighth-grade Students' Introspections of Discussions in Science and Social Studies Lessons. In J. A. Niles & R. V. Lalik (Eds.), *Issues in Literacy: A Research Perspective*. Thirty-fourth Yearbook of the National Reading Conference. Rochester, NY: National Reading Conference.

Davidson, Jane L. (1982). The Group Mapping Activity for Instruction in Reading and Thinking. *Journal of Reading*, vol. 26, pp. 52-56.

Davidson, Jane L. (1978). The DR-TA: A Reading-thinking Strategy for All Levels. In R. T. Vacca & J. A. Meagher (Eds.), *Reading as a Language-Experience*. Storrs, CT: Reading-Study Center, Dept. of Elementary Education, University of Connecticut, pp. 37-43.

Davidson, Jane L. (1970). *The Relationship Between Teachers' Questions and Pupils' Responses During a Directed Reading Activity and a Directed Reading-Thinking Activity*. Unpublished Ph.D. dissertation, University of Michigan.

Davidson, Jane L.; Padak, Nancy D.; and Wilkerson, Bonnie C. (1987). *Reconsidering a Focus for Curriculum Development: Curricular Issues*. Paper presented at the American Educational Research Association Conference, Washington, DC, April, 1987.

Davidson, Jane L.; Padak, Nancy D.; & Wilkerson, Bonnie C. (1986a). *Four Instructional Lessons in Science: The Process of Comprehension Attainment of Text*. Paper presented at the meeting of the International Reading Association, Philadelphia, PA.

Davidson, Jane L.; Padak, Nancy D.; & Wilkerson, Bonnie C. (1986b). *Instructional*

Frameworks in Junior High Science and Social Studies: How Lessons Evolve. Paper presented at the meeting of the American Educational Research Association, San Francisco, CA.

Davidson, Jane L.; Padak, Nancy D.; & Wilkerson, Bonnie C. (1986c). *Instructional Frameworks in Junior High Science and Social Studies: The Hidden Curriculum.* Paper presented at the meeting of the American Educational Research Association, San Francisco, CA.

Draheim, Marilyn. (1984). Facilitating Comprehension and Written Recall of Exposition Through DR-TA Instruction and Conceptual Mapping. In J. A. Niles (Ed.) and L. A. Harris (Assoc. Ed.), *Changing Perspectives on Research in Reading/Language Processing and Instruction.* Rochester, NY: National Reading Conference, pp. 167-172.

Duffy, G. (1981). Teacher Effectiveness Research: Implications for the Reading Profession. In M. Kamil (Ed.), *Directions in Reading: Research and Instruction.* Washington, DC: The National Reading Conference, pp. 113-135.

Durkin, Dolores (1978-79). What Classroom Observations Reveal about Reading Comprehension Instruction. *Reading Research Quarterly*, vol. 14, (4), pp. 481-533.

Green, Judith L. & Harker, J.O. (1982). Gaining Access to Learning: Conversational, Social, and Cognitive Demands of Group Participation. In L.C. Wilkinson (Ed.), *Communicating in the Classroom*, pp. 183-221. New York: Academic Press.

Grobler, C. van Eyk (1970). *Methodology in Reading Instruction as a Controlled Variable in the Constructive or Destructive Channeling of Aggression.* Unpublished Ph.D. dissertation, University of Delaware.

Guthrie, John T. (1979). Grouping for Reading: Research Views. *The Reading Teacher*, vol. 32, pp. 500-501.

Hammond, W. Dorsey (1979). *The Effects of Reader Predictions on Prequestions in the Recall of Relevant and Incidental Information Found in Expository Material.* A paper presented at the International Reading Association Annual Convention, Atlanta, GA., May.

Henderson, Edmund H. (1963). *Study of Individually Formulated Purposes for Reading in Relation to Reading Achievement Comprehension and Purpose Attainment.* Unpublished Ph.D. dissertation, University of Delaware, 1963.

Homer, Cynthia L. (1977). *The Influence on Reading Behavior of Two Purpose-Set-*

ting Procedures for Administering an Informal Reading Inventory. Unpublished Ed.D. dissertation, Northern Illinois University.

Horn, Ernest V. (1937). *Methods of Instruction in the Social Studies*. New York: Scribner.

Leavitt, H. J. (1958). *Managerial Psychology*. University of Chicago Press.

Lia, Douglas V. (1988). *A Study of Second Grade Students' Inferences During and Following Participation in Three Types of Read Aloud Story Sessions*. Unpublished Ed.D. dissertation, Northern Illinois University.

Manzo, Anthony V. & Sherk, Jr., John K. (1978). Reading and Languaging in the Content Areas. *New England Journal of Reading*. vol. 12. pp. 28-32.

McCracken, Robert A. (1966). *Standard Reading Inventory*. Klamath Falls, Oregon: Klamath Printing Co.

Padak, Nancy D. (1982). *An Analysis of the Quantity, Quality, and Variety of Inferences Generated During Directed Reading-Thinking Activities and Group Mapping Activities*. Paper presented at the National Reading Conference, Clearwater Beach, Florida.

Padak, Nancy D. (1987). *A Comparative Analysis of the Teacher's Roles in Two Junior High Literature Lessons*. Paper presented at the American Educational Research Association Conference, Washington, DC, April.

Padak, Nancy D. (1986). Teachers' Verbal Behaviors: A Window to the Teaching Process. In J. A. Niles & R. V. Lalik (Eds.), *Solving Problems in Literacy: Learners, Teachers, & Researchers*. Rochester, NY: National Reading Conference.

Padak, Nancy D. (1985). *A Teacher's Verbal Patterns and Decision-Making: The Influence of Instructional Setting*. Paper presented at the meeting of the American Educational Research Association, Chicago,IL.

Padak, Nancy D. & Padak, Gary (1987). Students' and Teachers' Perceptions of an Innovative Strategy. In J. E. Readence and R. S. Baldwin (Eds.), *Research as Literacy: Emerging Perspectives*. Rochester, NY: National Reading Conference.

Padak, Nancy D., & Davidson, Jane L. (1988a). *Inquiry Reading Instructional Activities for Facilitating the Process of Comprehension of Science Texts*. Unpublished paper, Kent, OH: Kent State University.

79

Padak, Nancy D., & Davidson, Jane L. (1988b). *What Are We Supposed to Do? Classroom Interactions and the Hidden Curriculum.* Unpublished paper, Kent, OH: Kent State University.

Petre, Richard M. (1969). *The Quantity, Quality, and Variety of Pupil Responses During an Open-communication Structured Group Directed Reading-thinking Activity and a Closed-communication Structured Directed Reading Activity.* Unpublished Ph.D. dissertation, University of Delaware, 1969.

Pinter, Karen. (1985). *The Effect of Text Simplification and Instructional Procedure on the Inference Generation of Fifth Grade Disabled Readers.* Unpublished Ed.D. dissertation, Northern Illinois University.

Rusnak, Martha. (1983). *The Relationship Between Teachers' Questions and Students' Responses During a Directed Reading-Thinking Activity and a Directed Reading Activity.* Unpublished Ed.D. dissertation, Northern Illinois University.

Smith, Frank. (1975). *Comprehension and Learning.* New York: Holt, Rinehart and Winston.

Spache, George (1968). Contributions of Allied Fields to the Teaching of Reading. *Innovations and Change in Reading Instruction.* Sixty-seventh Yearbook of the National Society for the Study of Education, Part II. Chicago: University of Chicago Press.

Stauffer, Russell G. (1980). *The Language-Experience Approach to the Teaching of Reading* (2nd ed.). NY: Harper & Row.

Stauffer, Russel G. (1975). *Directing the Reading-Thinking Process.* New York: Harper and Row Publishers.

Stauffer, Russell G. (1970). *The Language Experience Approach to the Teaching of Reading.* New York: Harper & Row Publishers.

Stauffer, Russell G. (1969). *Teaching Reading As a Thinking Process.* New York: Harper & Row Publishers.

Stauffer, Russell G. & Hammond, W. Dorsey (1969). Effectiveness of a Language Arts and Basic Reader Approach to First Grade Reading Instruction—Extended into Third Grade. *Reading Research Quarterly.* Vol. IV., (4), Summer, 1969.

Stauffer, Russell G., & Hammond, W. Dorsey (1966). *Effectiveness of a Language Arts and Basic Reader Approach to First Grade Reading Instruction—Extended into Second Grade.* (Final Report, Cooperative Research Project No. 3276) Newark, DE.: University of Delaware.

Stauffer, Russell G. & Hammond, W. Dorsey (1965). *Effectiveness of a Language Arts and Basic Reader Approach to First Grade Reading Instruction.* (Final Report, Cooperative Research Project No. 2679). Newark, DE.: University of Delaware.

Stauffer, Russell G., Hammond, W. Dorsey, Oehlkers, William J., Houseman, Anne. (1976). Effectiveness of a Language Arts and Basic Reader Approach to First Grade Reading Instruction—Extended into Sixth Grade. In R. G. Stauffer (Ed.), *Action Research in L.E.A. Instructional Procedures.* Newark, DE.: University of Delaware, 1976. pp. 166-203.

Taba, Hilda (1964). *Thinking in Elementary School Children.* U.S. Office of Education Cooperative Research Project (No. 1575), San Francisco State College, April.

Taba, Hilda (1962). *Curriculum Development: Theory and Practice.* New York: Harcourt, Brace and World.

Vygotsky, L. S. (1962). *Thought and Language.* New York: John Wiley and Sons, Inc.

Wilkerson, Bonnie C. (1987). *A Comparison of Student Inferencing Behavior in Literature Lessons and Student Inferencing Behavior in Science and Social Studies Lessons.* Paper presented at the American Educational Research Association Conference, Washington, DC, April.

Wilkerson, Bonnie C. (1986). Inferences: A Window to Comprehension. In J. A. Niles & R. V. Lalik (Eds.), *Solving Problems in Literacy: Learners, Teachers, & Researchers.* Rochester, NY: National Reading Conference.

Wilkerson, Bonnie C. (1984). *A Study of Students' Inferences During and Following a Group Directed Reading-Thinking Activity and a Group Directed Reading Activity in Social Studies.* Unpublished doctoral dissertation, Northern Illinois University, DeKalb.

Wolf, W., King, M., & Huck, C. (1967). *Critical Reading Ability of Elementary School Children.* U.S. Office of Education Cooperative Research Project (No. 5-1040). Ohio State University, June.

Zeichner, Kenneth. (1979) In J. T. Guthrie, Grouping for Reading: Research Views. *The Reading Teacher*, vol. 32, pp. 500-501.